Active
Grammar

W-D. Bald
D. J. Cobb
A. Schwarz

Longman

Longman Group Limited,
Longman House, Burnt Mill, Harlow,
Essex CM20 2JE, England
and Associated Companies throughout the world.

First published © Langenscheidt-Longman 1984 GmbH, Munich
English monolingual edition © Longman Group Limited 1986

This edition first published 1986
Second impression 1986
Third impression 1986
ISBN 0 582 51738 9

Illustrated by Erhard Dietl and David Mostyn

Acknowledgments

The authors are grateful to the following consultants
for their advice on many points:
W. Hüllen, H.-E. Piepho, S. Chalker and R. A. Close.
   Where their advice could not always be followed in
every detail and where as a result it may be thought
that there are omissions, or generalizations and
simplifications which are too extreme, the authors
acknowledge that the responsibility is entirely their own.

We are grateful to the following for permission to reproduce copyright material: Erhard Dietl, Munchen for pages 9, 21, 30, 36
(top), 49, 50, 55, 57 (bottom), 58, 60, 61, 68, 71, 73, 77, 78, 80, 81, 90, 92, 96, 99, 100, 103, 104, 108, 110, 112, 113, 114, 115,
118, 120, 121, 125, 129, 130, 131, 136, 137 & 138; Tony Goffe (by permission of Linda Rogers Associates) for pages 2 & 8;
William P. Hoest, New York for pages 41, 43, 70, 74, 75 & 116; Kipper Williams for pages 56 & 94 (top); London Express News
and Feature Services for page 3; taken from The Book of British Humour, compiled by J. King, R. Ridout, D. K. Swan ©
Longman Group Ltd. for pages 14, 18, 35, 59 & 89; taken from Longman Active Study Dictionary of English © Longman Group
Ltd. for page 126; Reproduced by permission of Punch for page 4; STERN-magazine/Hamburg for page 57 (top); Mirror Group
Newspapers/Syndication International Ltd. for pages 6, 20, 42 & 52; United Feature Syndicate Inc., New York for page 111,
taken from Grasping Grammar © Wolters-Noordhoff-Longman for page 36 (bottom).

Set in Helvetica Light
by MFK Typesetting, Saffron Walden

Printed in Great Britain by
Butler & Tanner Ltd, Frome and London.

CONTENTS

THE SENTENCE

THE PARTS OF THE SENTENCE

COMMUNICATIVE SITUATIONS

Abbreviations and symbols

Adj	Adjective	i.e.	that is
Adv	Adverb	N	Noun
Aux	Auxiliary, helping verb	O$_d$	Direct object
AmE	American English	O$_i$	Indirect object
BrE	British English	S	Subject
Conj	Conjunction	V	Verb
e.g.	for example	=	means
etc.	etcetera/and so on		

Phonetic symbols

Pronunciation throughout this book is shown in the system used in the Longman *Active Study Dictionary* and *Dictionary of Contemporary English*. The symbols are shown in this table, with a key word for each. The letters printed in bold type represent the sound value of each symbol.

Consonants

§ /p/	pen	§* /s/	soon
+/b/	back	+*/z/	zero
§ /t/	tea	§* /ʃ/	fishing
+/d/	day	+*/ʒ/	pleasure
§ /k/	key	/h/	hot
+/g/	gay	/m/	sum
* /tʃ/	cheer	/n/	sun
* /dʒ/	jump	/ŋ/	sung
§ /f/	few	/l/	led
+/v/	view	/r/	red
§ /θ/	thing	/j/	yet
+/ð/	then	/w/	wet

Vowels

/iː/	sheep
/ɪ/	ship
/e/	bed
/æ/	bad
/ɑː/	calm
/ɒ/	pot
/ɔː/	caught
/ʊ/	put
/uː/	boot
/ʌ/	cut
/ɜː/	bird
/ə/	cupboard

Diphthongs

/eɪ/	make
/aɪ/	bite
/əʊ/	note
/aʊ/	now
/ɔɪ/	boy
/ɪə/	here
/eə/	there
/ʊə/	poor
/eɪə/	player
/əʊə/	lower
/aɪə/	tire
/aʊə/	tower
/ɔɪə/	employer

Consonants marked * are *sibilants*
Consonants marked § are *voiceless*
Consonants marked + are *voiced*

The alphabet

a	b	c	d	e	f	g	h	i	j	k	l	m
/eɪ/	/biː/	/siː/	/diː/	/iː/	/ef/	/dʒiː/	/eɪtʃ/	/aɪ/	/dʒeɪ/	/keɪ/	/el/	/em/

n	o	p	q	r	s	t	u	v	w	x	y	z
/en/	/əʊ/	/piː/	/kjuː/	/ɑː/	/es/	/tiː/	/juː/	/viː/	/dʌbljuː/	/eks/	/waɪ/	/zed/

Stress and intonation

Capitals = nuclear stress in a statement (It was SANdra.)

= stressed syllable (Her 'mother said NO.)

= falling intonation tune (Never!)

= rising intonation tune (When?)

= the intonation first falls and then rises again (Mary?)

FOREWORD

After about two or three years, or 150–180 hours of instruction, students usually reach the pre-intermediate stage of learning. From this point onwards they need a simple grammar to refer to. Such a grammar helps them to consolidate what they have learnt, and to organize it into a system.

This is exactly the purpose of *Active Grammar*. It describes those aspects of English grammar and usage which are generally covered in the syllabus of a modern English language course at the beginners' and pre-intermediate levels.

Keeping in mind the students' still rather limited experience of English, all explanations are kept as simple as possible. This applies both to the actual wording of the explanations and the depth to which any grammatical feature is treated.

Active Grammar provides two points of entry by which students can find what they want to look up: *the contents list* at the front of the book, which arranges grammatical features and communicative functions in sections of related topics; and *the index* at the back of the book, which lists the same grammatical features and communicative functions in alphabetical order, at the same time adding most of the key structural words and examples which are printed bold in the explanatory text. Cross-referencing is used extensively, in both index and text, to maximize the chances that students will find what they are looking for.

Active Grammar covers both spoken and written forms of English. However, the main emphasis is on everyday spoken English suited to the needs of students at the pre-intermediate and intermediate levels. Throughout the book, form and use are carefully related, and there are also special sections to show how a variety of communicative purposes can be achieved.

In short, *Active Grammar* aims at helping students to *use* English grammatically and communicatively, not just to *know about* grammar. The majority of students will, however, still need a lot of practice before they are confident and fluent in their use of even fairly basic English. For this reason, we recommend highly use of *Active Grammar Exercises* as an ideal companion to this grammar.

THE SENTENCE

1 The simple sentence

A simple sentence consists of two parts: a subject and a predicate. It does not have any dependent clauses. It may take one of four different forms: a statement, a question, an imperative, or an exclamation. Each of these four different types of simple sentence has its own structure, as the following notes explain.

1.1 Statements

1.1.1. Word order in statements

Subject S	Auxiliary verb Aux	Verb V	Object O	Adverb Adv
My friend	will	send	a letter.	
I		telephoned	him	(today).
He		agreed		(immediately).
The office	had	forgotten	our order.	

The core of the sentence is S+Aux+V+O. In English this sequence is followed strictly in almost all statements. (You can find exceptions in 1.4.3, where you will see that these follow a small number of strict rules.)

Adverbs may appear in various positions in the statements (see 1.1.11 to 1.1.13), but the end of the sentence is a common position.

The examples in the table show that a sentence does not necessarily contain all the possible parts. The core of the sentence, for instance, may be either S+V, or S+V+O, or S+Aux+V+O.

It is the verb which generally determines the parts of the sentence that are represented.

1.1.2 Different kinds of subjects

S	
Mary	left the shop.
Coffee	was very expensive.
The funny little shop	had almost everything.
She	forgot to buy milk.

There is a variety of possible subjects in a sentence. This includes proper names, pronouns, and nouns which may or may not have other words attached to them.

S	
Swimming	can be dangerous.
But collecting stamps	is very safe.

We may use the *verb base + **ing*** as a subject (see 1.1.3.1).

S	
To see her	was a great surprise.
To leave so early	seemed very unfriendly.

We may also use the *infinitive* of a verb, with **to** in front of it, as a subject (see 1.1.3.2 and 2.3.12), but note that sentences of the type It was a great surprise to see her. are more common in everyday English (see *cleft sentence* 2.3.14).

1.1.3 Kinds of object

V	O	
Bill met	**Jack**	early in the morning.
They planned	**a safari**	to Africa.
Bill photographed	**the biggest animals still alive.**	
The party climbed	**Mount Everest**	in 1976.

There is a close relationship between verb and object in a sentence. As a rule no other part of the sentence comes between them.

Common kinds of object are proper names, nouns with or without other words attached to them, and pronouns.

1.1.3.1 Verb base + ing*

	O
I like	all kinds of sport.
But I dislike	**jogging.**
Mary enjoys	**playing** hockey.
John hates	**dancing.**

In addition to these, we may use *verb base + **ing*** as an object. Certain verbs (**avoid, deny, enjoy, finish, keep on, stop** = 'finish doing something') frequently have *verb base + **ing*** as an object. (Idioms with *verb base + **ing*** – see 2.3.13. *Verb base + **ing*** as subject – see 1.1.2).

*Many grammars used to call this form the *gerund*.

I am	**fond of**	**camping** in England.
Eva	**succeeded in**	**getting** to New York.
There are	many **chances of**	**meeting** new people.
She is	**good at**	**learning** new languages.

Another use of *verb base* + **ing** is after

Adjectives	
Verbs	+ prepositions.
Nouns	

Spelling rules:
a) double the final consonant if the vowel is stressed and written as a single letter, and also if there is only a single final consonant. So:
get → getting, **sit → sitting**, but **head → heading**, **mend → mending**
b) **ie** in front of **ing** becomes **y**:
die → dying, **lie → lying**.

1.1.3.2 Infinitives

	O
Alison preferred	**to leave**.
She wanted	**to meet** her friend.
They'd like	**to go** by plane.

What do you do on Sundays?	– I **like watching** TV.
What are your plans for tonight?	– I **would like to watch** TV.
I **love dancing**, but this evening I'**d prefer to sit** here quietly: I don't feel very well.	

We can also sometimes use the infinitives of verbs + **to** as objects. The infinitive may have other words with it. But the verbs we listed at 1.1.3.1 (**stop***, etc.) cannot have infinitives as objects.

Most verbs which we use to talk about our likes and dislikes and preferences, such as **hate**, **(dis)like**, **love**, **prefer** (but not **enjoy**) may have either *verb base* + **ing** or an *infinitive* + **to** after them. But the meaning changes: we use *base* + **ing** to talk about habits, but infinitives to refer to an event on a certain occasion and at a particular moment in time. Verbs in this group (**like**, **love**, etc.) are often used in the base form with **would** ('**d**) in front of them, i.e. **would** + *base* + **to** *infinitive*.

3

'How humiliating – personally I would rather borrow or steal!'

Remember the special case of **I'd rather** + *infinitive without* **to**, which expresses preferences, e.g. I'd rather drink coffee than tea.

He stopped smoking.	(He had the habit of smoking, but he gave it up.)
He stopped to smoke.	(He stopped what he was doing so that he could have a smoke).
He remembered to ask the question.	(He remembered something he needed to do and did it.)
He remembered asking the question.	(He remembered something which had happened on a previous occasion.)

*We must also take special note of the verb **stop**, whose meaning changes if it is followed by an *infinitive* + **to** instead of a *verb base* + **ing**.

The verbs **remember** and **forget** may be followed by *infinitive* + **to**, but have a different meaning if followed by *verb base* + **ing**.

1.1.4 Two objects

S	Aux	V	Indirect object O$_i$	Direct object O$_d$
We	will	send	you	more information.
They	didn't	show	Mary	the way.

Some verbs, like **send, give, show**, can have two objects. The indirect object comes before the direct object: $O_i - O_d$

		O$_i$		O$_d$
Roger	gave	Sally		a nice present.
Roger	gave	a nice present	to	Sally. (not to Mary!)
		O$_d$	**to**	O$_i$

Sometimes we need to place special emphasis on the *indirect object*. We then put it after the direct object, with the preposition **to** in front of it: $O_d - $ **to** $ - O_i$. In speaking, we would probably put some stress on **to** + *indirect object*.

The most important information, things which the listener is hearing for the first time or which we want to emphasize, is usually found at the end of an English sentence. So, by choosing between the two orders of objects ($O_i - O_d$, or $O_d - \boldsymbol{to} - O_i$) we can emphasize the object which contains the more important information for the person we are talking (or writing) to.

What's going on here?
Did you give the dog my SAUSAGE?

– No, I gave it your CAKE!

John, did you give my sausage to the DOG?

– No, I gave it to the CAT!

In this example, the *direct object* is the main topic of conversation. It therefore appears last in both question and answer. Stress and the falling intonation tune reinforce the choice of the pattern $O_i - O_d$.

Here, in this second example, it is the *indirect object* which is the main topic of conversation. We have chosen the pattern $O_d - O_i$ so that the indirect object now comes last. This time, stress and the falling-rising intonation tune reinforce the pattern.

Could you send **it to** the company?
Could you show **them to** us?

If the direct object is **it** or **them**, we normally follow the pattern $O_d - \boldsymbol{to} - O_i$.

	O_d	**to** O_i
The policeman **described**	the way	to the campers.
He **explained**	the map	to them.

With the verb **describe** we can use only the pattern $O_d - \boldsymbol{to} - O_i$, and with **explain** we often use the same pattern.

Alison	**said** (to her mother)	that she had lost the way.
She	**explained** (to her mother)	that she had lost the way.
She	**told her (mother)**	that she had lost the way.
She	**told the story**	**to her (mother)**.

Say and **tell**:
If the verb **say** has an indirect object, this always follows the word **to**. We can use the verb **tell**, which normally needs an indirect object, in both patterns, $O_i - O_d$ and $O_d - \boldsymbol{to} - O_i$. We can also use **explain** like **say** in this pattern.

5

'Have you told them about my spots?'

1.1.5 Position of auxiliary verbs

	Aux	V	
The children	**will**	travel	to London soon.
They	**have been**	looking forward	to this journey.
It	**might have been**	stopped	at the last moment.

We put auxiliary verbs immediately in front of the main verb. This is still true even if there is more than one auxiliary verb.

1.1.6 Use of simple sentences

We can find typical examples of the use of simple sentences in summaries, news headlines and in brief explanations. In these, the most important information is often found at the ends of sentences. For this reason, the *nuclear stress* is often found in the same position.

The 'text is about the 'world in the FUture. It has 'three PARTS. The 'first part deals with 'plants and

ANimals. The 'second describes PEOPle, and the 'third is about 'people from a'nother STAR.

We also hear simple sentences in sports commentaries:
'Robson crosses the ball to 'MARiner. Mariner heads it on to 'BARNES.
Barnes scores a tremendous 'GOAL!'

1.1.7 Passive sentences

Sentences with verbs in the passive are very common in reports of events, such as news items. If the reporter does not know what (or who) caused the event to happen, it is often better to use the passive instead of a rather meaningless subject, like **people** or **somebody**. And sometimes, even if the reporter does know the cause or agent, he prefers not to mention it. A sentence may then have only the following parts:
– the subject, to which something happens,
– the verb (part of the verb **be** in the appropriate tense, and a past participle),
– any adverbials that are needed.

	S	Form of **be** + past participle	Adv, etc.
Past	Two government officials	**were suspended**	from their posts in June.
Past perfect	This was because some important secrets	**had been given**	to the press.
Present perfect	Since June, several government buildings	**have been set**	on fire.
Present progressive	The causes of these fires	**are** (still) **being investigated**	by the police.
Present	Little	**is known**	so far.
Future	However, a press conference	**will be held**	this evening.
Modal auxiliary	Photographs	**may be had**	from the police.

Active	S	V		O
	The police rescued			the driver.
	The driver was rescued			by the police.
Passive	S	Form of **be** + past participle		**by** + agent

Comparison of active and passive:

The subject of an active sentence can be included in the corresponding passive sentence too, if we add it to the end of the sentence with the preposition **by**. (It is then called the 'agent' of the action.) Including the agent makes it seem important, so we must be sure we really need it. The subject of a passive sentence is the object in the corresponding active sentence.

'Are you married?'
'No, it's not that. I've been run over by a car!'

1.1.8 Passive with two objects

Passive	Active
Mary was given **the stamps**. **The stamps** were given **to Mary**.	Someone gave Mary the stamps.
John was sent **the money**. **The money** was sent **to John**.	Someone sent John the money.

We can form two different passive sentences from one active sentence, if the verb in the active sentence has two objects (see 1.1.4). This is because either the direct object or the indirect object in the active sentence can become the subject of the passive sentence.

S		O_i

Someone gave **her** the stamps.

↓ ↓

She was given the stamps. The stamps were given to **her**.

Remember that subject pronouns are different from direct object pronouns.

Active	Passive
The farmer described the way to the boys.	→ The way was described to the boys.
The teacher explained the formula to the class.	→ The formula was explained to the class.

There is only one way of making a passive sentence if it has a verb which is used in the pattern O_d – **to** – O_i (see 1.1.4).

Active	Passive
People looked down upon Fred.	→ Fred was **looked down upon**.
People even laughed at him.	→ He was even **laughed at**.
A car ran him over.	→ He's been **run over**.

Strawberries are often eaten with cream.
You often eat strawberries with cream.
People often eat strawberries with cream.
(One often eats strawberries with cream.)

Special care is needed with *phrasal verbs*, that is, verbs which have a preposition or adverbial particle attached to the main verb. In passive sentences, the preposition or adverbial particle always comes immediately after the main verb.

We can use impersonal subjects (**you**, **people**, **one**) to make active sentences with meanings that correspond to passive sentences that have no agent. But avoid using **one** as much as possible, because many people now consider this odd style.

1.1.9 Use of the passive

Ten people **were arrested** when the house **was searched**. Several people **have been accused** of various offences. The press **have been asked** not to disclose details so long as enquiries continue.

The passive is chosen when the agent or cause of an action or event is unknown, or is too unimportant or obvious to be worth mentioning, or should not be mentioned for some reason. Passive sentences are therefore very common in newspaper reports of accidents, crimes, etc.

   The most important or surprising information is often kept to the end of an English sentence (see 1.1.4). You will see in the joke opposite that using the passive is a way of producing a surprise at the end of a sentence, i.e. the funniness of being knocked down by a pram comes out stronger in I was knocked down **by a pram**. than it would have been in **A pram** knocked me down!

'What happened to you?' –
'You will never believe this.
I was knocked down by a pram.'

1.1.10 Passive with *get*

> Many people **get lost** in New York every year; some even **get killed**.

The passive is usually made with one or other form of the verb **be**, but we can also use the verb **get**.

We use this form of the passive to put emphasis on the result of an action or event. Some past participles cannot be combined with **get**, but the following combinations are very common: **get married/ broken/killed/lost/hurt/burnt**.

The use of **get** in the passive is more common in spoken English than in the written language.

1.1.11 Position of adverbials: final position

The position of adverbials* in an English sentence depends on (a) the form and meaning of the adverbial itself (b) the structure of the sentence in which it appears, and finally (c) the emphasis the writer or speaker chooses to give to it in his communication. (For the formation of adverbials, see 4.4.1.)

S	V	O	Adv
Your parcel	arrived		**safely**.
I	listened	to the record	**carefully**.
John Williams	plays	the guitar	**beautifully**.
He	interprets	the music	**in a very personal way**.

Adverbials of manner normally come at the end of a sentence (= in final position). They answer the question **How ...?**

S	V	Adv
He	spoke	**calmly**.
The patient	breathed	**in short gasps**.

If a sentence consists only of *S + V* and an adverbial of manner, the adverbial tends to come at the end.

*Adverbials may be only a single word (e.g. **naturally**) or they may be several words (e.g. **in a natural way**). The former are often called *adverbs* and the latter *adverbial phrases*. But in this section we use the term *adverbial* to cover both, as their function in the sentence is the same.

S	V	O	Adv
The inspector	opened	the door	slowly.
The inspector	**slowly**	opened	the door.
S	Adv	V	O

But if the sentence has other parts (e.g. *O*) in addition to *S + V*, we may place single word adverbials of manner, e.g. **quickly**, **slowly**, **anxiously**, **carefully**, not only at the end of the sentence, but also between subject and verb.

S	V	O	Adv
The boy scouts	left	their camp	**yesterday.**
They	had packed	their things	**early in the morning.**
They all	walked		**to the next village.**
A bus	was waiting		**there.**

Adverbials of time and *place*, on the other hand, normally come only at the ends of sentences. *Adverbials of time* answer the questions **When?** or **What time?** and *adverbials of place* answer the questions **Where (to)?** or **Which way?**

(For the functions of **there**, see 3.8.3.)

	Manner	Place	Time
Columbus	sailed		**to America**	**500 years ago.**
He	arrived	**safely**		**in October 1492.**
The Red Indians	waited	**anxiously**	**on the shore**	**during the landing.**

If there are several different adverbials in the same sentence they usually appear in the order *Manner – Place – Time.*

He arrived **at five o'clock on Monday**.
His family was waiting for him **at the ticket office inside the station**.

If there are two adverbials of the same type, the more particular one normally comes before the more general one.

We were in Venice yesterday and are in Florence today. **Tomorrow** we shall leave for Rome.
Last Christmas Day I was feeling rather sorry for myself, when there was a knock at the door.

Note that we may put *adverbials of time* at the beginning of a sentence, if we want to make a contrast, or set a scene (see 1.1.14).

11

1.1.12 Position of adverbials: medial position

S	Adv	V	O
The dog	**always**	accompanied	them.
They	**often**	hunted	rabbits.
Their neighbours	**sometimes**	saw	a few foxes.

S	V	Adv	
They	meet	**weekly**.	

	1. Aux	Adv	2. Aux	V	
You	can	**always**		ask	a policeman.
We	wouldn't	**ever**	have	found	the place.
It	was	**really**			a surprise.

Adverbs of frequency, such as **always, generally, never, often, rarely, usually** refer directly to the verb and are placed immediately in front of it, i.e. between *S* and *V*. This is called the *medial position*.

On the other hand, **annually, monthly, weekly, yearly** always appear at the end.

If there is an auxiliary verb in the sentence, adverbs in medial position are placed after the first auxiliary (or in negative statements auxiliary + negative; see 1.4).

We always treat **be** and its various forms as auxiliaries, i.e. adverbs come after them.

1.1.13 Immediate pre-position of adverbials

The team looked **quite fit**.
They **definitely wanted** to win.
They entered the playground **very slowly**.
Hardly anyone spoke.

Adverbs of degree, such as **definitely, hardly, just, quite, scarcely, thoroughly, very**, are placed immediately before the word or words which they modify.

He had **just** arrived.

Note that it is incorrect to place the adverbs **just**, **never** at the end of a sentence.

1.1.14 Use of adverbials

The usual place for adverbials of time and place is at the end of the sentence. But we may also put them at the beginning, and then we give them special emphasis and stress. The intonation tune changes accordingly.

His 'sister went to LONdon yesterday.

YESterday his 'sister went to LONdon; toDAY she is ex'pected in EDinburgh.

Adverbials which usually appear in medial position may also be placed at the beginning of a sentence, if we want to emphasize them:

Do you ever visit your grandparents? – Oh, I go SOMEtimes.

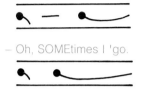

– Oh, SOMEtimes I 'go.

1.1.15 Sentence adverbials

> **Frankly**, I hate fish.
> I hate fish, **frankly**.
> **Naturally**, he behaved (well) among his friends.
> **Of course**, she never really told the whole truth.
> But:
> He behaved **naturally** among his friends.

NOTES
If we use the adverbials **never**, **hardly**, **rarely**, **scarcely** to modify verbs and put them at the beginning of a sentence for emphasis, *inversion* takes place. But we do not do this with sentences containing only $S + Adv + V$ (see 1.4.3).

Sentence adverbials refer to the whole sentence, not just a part of it. They tell us the speaker's attitude to the statement he is about to make (or has just made). They usually come at the beginning of the sentence, but sometimes at the end. In writing, we separate them from the rest of the sentence with a comma; in speaking, by a short pause. For this reason, they receive independent stress when we say them aloud. If these rules are observed, no confusion can occur between sentence adverbials and adverbials which refer to just one part of the sentence.

1.2 Questions

In English there are various different ways of asking questions. We can classify them according to the kinds of answer which we expect:

Yes/No questions (e.g. Are you leaving?) These expect the listener (or reader) to state his decision, **Yes** or, **No**.

Alternative questions (with **or**) (e.g. Would you like tea or coffee?). These expect the listener to choose between the alternatives mentioned (e.g. by saying **Coffee, please.**)

Wh-questions are open-ended. These expect the listener to answer by giving some information. (For *indirect questions*, see 2.3.11.)

(Of course, we can avoid answering all three kinds of questions by saying something like **I don't know** or **I'm not sure.**)

1.2.1 *Yes/No* questions

Aux	S	V (infin- itive)	O/Adj/Adv, etc.	
May	I	have	some more tea?	– Yes, of course.
Would	you	like	some sugar?	– No, thank you.
Is	it		too strong for you?	– No, it's perfect.
Could	we	plan	our party now?	– OK, fine.

Aux	S	V	O/Adj/Adv
Have	you	(got)	a car?
Has	he	had	a bath yet?
Had	they	seen	the film before?

Aux	S	V	O/Adj/Adv		
Do	you	know	about cars?	– Of course.	Present
Does	your family	want	a jeep?	– Oh, yes.	
Did	your father	sell	his car?	– Yes, he did.	Past

Did he **lose** his money?   – No, he **lost** his key.
Does Mary look happy?   – No, she look**s** very unhappy.

Billy didn't ask for a cake. He simply reached across the table and took one.
'Billy!' said his mother sharply. 'Haven't you got a tongue in your mouth?'
'Yes, Mum,' Billy replied. 'But it won't reach as far as the cakes.'

In Britain, especially:
Have you got a 10p coin?
Have you got the time? (i.e. Can you tell me what the time is now?)

In America, especially:
Do you have a dime?
Do you have the time?

But in both Britain and America:
Do you (ever/often) have toothache?

Yes/No questions always begin with an auxiliary verb, which of course includes **be**. In other words, inversion takes place. After the auxiliary, the other parts of the sentence follow in the sequence *S + base form (+ object/adjective/ adverbial, if any)*.

Have may also be used as an auxiliary. The verb in the third box is then not an infinitive; it is either a past participle (perfect tenses), or in the case of **have got** may disappear altogether, e.g. Have you a car?

If the auxiliary in first position is not a form of **be, have** or a modal, e.g. **can, must,** we use the appropriate tense and form of **do (does, did).**

When you answer a **Yes/No** question, you must be careful to get the tense right, and to put **s** on the third person singular of the present tense. For it is the auxiliary verb which bears the responsibility for showing number, person and tense, e.g. Does your brother play tennis? – Yes, he does.

NOTES
The British prefer **have got** when they are talking about a particular moment (e.g. **now**), and **have** when they mean **at any time** (which in questions may be indicated by the word **ever**). Americans use **have got** much less, and so **have** may refer to a particular moment or time in general (see 3.9.2).

1.2.2 Use of *Yes/No* questions

Have you seen the NEIGHbours? – Yes.

Do you LIKE them? – Well, I don't know.

Questions made by inverting subject and auxiliary (i.e. *Aux + S + V* instead of *S + Aux + V*) anticipate the answer **Yes** or **No**. To underline this expectation we use a rising intonation tune.

1.2.3 Declarative questions

You came in very LATE last night? – Yes, that's true.

And you didn't lock the DOOR? – No, I didn't.

You aren't very good at MATHS? – No, I'm not.

Sometimes the parts of a sentence are kept in the same order as in a statement, and we are told only by the intonation tune that we should understand it as a question. Questions of this kind anticipate agreement.

Note that in English it is possible to agree with someone by saying **No** as well as **Yes**.

For example, the person answering the last question agrees that he is not very good at maths.

1.2.4 Tag questions

Jane **has** married a Swede, **hasn't** she?
They **were** married in Birmingham, **weren't** they?

They **won't** move to Sweden, **will** they?

You **forgot** their wedding day, **didn't** you?

A tag question is a short question added to the end of a statement to make it a question.

If there is an auxiliary, the tag consists of the same auxiliary in its opposite form, i.e. affirmative becomes negative (**has → hasn't**) and negative becomes affirmative (**won't → will**) and this is followed by the pronoun appropriate to the subject in the statement part of the sentence. (This may, of course, already be a pronoun, and in this event it is simply repeated.) **Jane → she, they → they**).

If the statement does not contain an auxiliary, we must supply the appropriate form of **do** in the tag. (**forgot → didn't**).

If I don't like it, I don't have to eat it, DO I?

Tag questions are colloquial in style and people use them mainly in conversation. They are like **Yes/No** questions (see 1.2.2) because they usually anticipate agreement.

Note that the following are irregular tag questions:
I'm your best friend, aren't I? (see 1.4.2)
Let's go, shall we? (see 1.3)

I could order something else, COULDn't I?

A tag question with a *falling* intonation tune anticipates agreement. Disagreement would be a surprise. But a tag question with a *rising* intonation tune tells us that the speaker is less certain the listener will agree with him (or her).

Your watch was slow again, WAS it?

So you missed the lesson once more, DID you?

Note that you will also hear (or see) some tag questions in which *both* parts are positive. This is a common way of making slightly ironic remarks about rather obvious facts. In this pattern the intonation tune always *rises*.

1.2.5 Alternative questions (with *or*)

Shall we go by BUS, by TRAIN or by CAR? – By bus, please.

If the intonation tune *falls* on the last of the possible choices offered, after being high on the preceding one or ones, we are told that these are in fact all the choices available. (In the example given, we should have misunderstood the situation if we answered Oh, let's take a TAXI. The questioner has already indicated that there are no taxis available, or that we cannot afford one.)

Do you want TEA or COFfee?   – Perhaps some milk?

If the intonation tune *rises* on all the possible choices given, we can understand that there are further possibilities which have not been named (perhaps **milk**, **lemonade**, etc.).

1.2.6 *Wh*-questions

S	(Aux) + V	O/Adv, etc.	
Who	came	for lunch?	– The Weavers.
What	(has) happened	to their car?	– I don't know.

Wh-word	Aux	S	V	O/Adv, etc.	
Where	are	we	going	today?	– To the Red Lion.
When	should	we	leave?		– About twelve.
What	**do**	they	serve	for dinner?	– I don't know.
Why	**didn't**	you	ask	them?	– Oh, I forgot.
How	can	one	forget	about food?	– You are greedy!

Whose grammar book have you got?	
Which dictionary did they buy?	

Whom ⎫	do you want to see?
Who ⎰	can we ask?

What are you looking **at**? – Oh, I wasn't looking **at** anything.
Then **what** were you thinking **of**? – Nothing, just dreaming.
Where does your friend come **from**? – He comes **from** Norway.

When the **Wh**-*question word* functions as the subject of the sentence (i.e. asks the listener to supply a new subject), the sentence keeps to the normal order of parts in a statement, *S + V + O*. We do not add any form of the verb **do**.

If the **Wh**-question word is not concerned with the subject, but asks about some other part of the sentence, then the order of parts after the **Wh**-word is the same as it is in **Yes/No** questions (see 1.2.1): *Aux + S + V + O*, etc.

Whose? and **Which?** may be used in front of nouns, like attributive adjectives (see 4.5.8).

We may use either **Whom**? or **Who**? to ask about objects of sentences, if they are persons. **Whom**? is more formal and now very uncommon in spoken English, and rather rare in written English too.

When **Who**? = **Whom**? it must, of course, be followed by an auxiliary. (For **Who**? as subject, see above.)

When sentences contain phrasal verbs, e.g. **come about** (= happen), **come from**, **listen to**, **look at**, **think of**, **watch out**, **write about**, adverbial particles or prepositions follow immediately after the main verb.

1.2.7 Intonation of *Wh*-questions

Wh-questions usually have a falling intonation tune.

1.3 Imperatives

	V	Adj/O/Adv
	Jump!	
But	be	careful.
	Take	a good look first.
	Don't lose	your shoes.
	Do not park	here.

You sit in the back, because I know the way.

Let's go now, the taxi is waiting.

Let's not waste our time.
Don't let's open the door.

The purpose of imperative sentences is to give commands, orders or instructions, or to make requests. The verb in imperative sentences is the *base form*, without a subject. The *negative imperative*, which functions as a warning, consists of **Do not/ Don't** + the *base form* of the verb.

You is sometimes added to the *base form*, for emphasis or to draw attention to the person addressed.

There is another kind of imperative, which uses **Let's/Let us.** This is more in the nature of an exhortation or a suggestion than a command, and the speaker is included in the course of action which he (or she) proposes.

The common negative forms of **Let's** are **Let's not** and **Don't let's.**

1.3.1 Use of imperatives

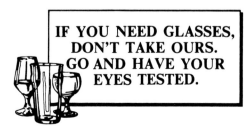

IF YOU NEED GLASSES, DON'T TAKE OURS. GO AND HAVE YOUR EYES TESTED.

Imperatives are used a great deal by parents to their young children, but adults discourage children from using them. This is because they may sound rather 'bossy'. To avoid the imperative, we may use certain auxiliaries which can have the same function (see also 5.5).

You can go now.
You may go now. } = Go.
We can go now.
Shall we go now? } = Let's go.
I don't think you should go yet.
You shouldn't go yet. } = Don't go.
Can I ask you to be quieter, please? = Please be quiet.

Don't forget your umBRELla, and take your 'coat, TOO.

DO TELL me, I MUST know her 'secret.

An imperative usually has a falling intonation tune.

Note that you can give additional emphasis to positive imperatives by adding **Do**, which is then often the most heavily stressed word in the sentence.

1.4 Negation

1.4.1 Negative statements

		Aux + **not**	V	
	He	could**n't**	sleep,	
but	he	had**n't**	seen	his doctor.
	He	was**n't**		the same any more.
Surely,	this	ca**n't**	be called	OK.
	Jack	does**n't**	trust	me.
	He	did**n't**	tell	me a single word.

Not (or its contracted form **n't** – see 1.4.2) is placed after the first auxiliary verb. Parts of the verb **be** are treated as auxiliary verbs.
    If the statement which we are negating does not contain an auxiliary, the appropriate form of **do** is used as an auxiliary and negated instead.

1.4.2 Contracted forms

cannot	can't
could not	couldn't
dare not	daren't
may not	(mayn't) (rare)
might not	mightn't
must not	mustn't
need not	needn't
ought not to	oughtn't to
shall not	shan't
should not	shouldn't
will not	won't.
would not	wouldn't
used not to	usedn't to
(or: did not	(or: didn't
use to)	use to)

do not	don't
does not	doesn't
did not	didn't
have not	haven't
has not	hasn't
had not	hadn't
am not	'm not*
are not	aren't
is not	isn't
was not	wasn't
were not	weren't

In spoken English, **not** is very often attached to the preceding auxiliary verb and contracted, i.e. shortened to **n't**. (For this purpose, auxiliary verbs include **do, have, be**.)

Contractions of **not** are less usual in written English, but are nevertheless very common in personal correspondence.

Some exceptions must be noted: We write **cannot** as one word; **shall not** and **will not** produce the irregular contracted forms, **shan't** and **won't**; **am not** contracts to **'m not**, e.g. I'm not leaving before Tom comes.

*NOTES
a) In tag questions **aren't I?** is used instead of **am not I?** e.g. I'm your best friend, aren't I?

b) If you come across people speaking British or American slang or local dialects, you will sometimes hear **ain't = am not** or **is not**. You should not copy them (unless perhaps you are singing a folk song or pop song, or you are an actor taking a Cockney part, for example.)

If we want to emphasize that our statement is negative, we do not shorten **not**, either in speech or in writing. (In the example opposite, it is clear that the TV announcer emphasized **not** when he spoke. Otherwise it would have been more appropriate to write **isn't**.)

'The next programme is not suitable for nervous viewers.'

1.4.3 Inversion after negative adverbials

	Aux	S	V	
Never	had	Tom	walked	as far as this.
But **hardly (scarcely)**	had	he	got	to the castle, when the rain started.
Rarely	had	he	seen	such floods come down.

If 'negative' adverbs, like **hardly**, **never**, **rarely**, **scarcely**, **seldom**, are put at the beginning of a statement, the order of the parts changes to that of a question: *Aux + S + V*. (This is called *inversion*.) If there is no auxiliary verb in the sentence, the appropriate part of the verb **do** is supplied instead (just as happens when we ask a question or make a negative statement). The examples given would not normally be heard in everyday English conversation. They are more typical of stories told to children, or of history books.

Hardly anyone saw what happened.

Note that inversion does *not* take place if **hardly**, **scarcely** change the meaning of the noun subject and not the verb.

	Aux + S

The cat did not obey, and **neither** did the dog! (. . . and the dog didn't obey, either.)
The boy can't train them, and **nor** can the girl. (. . . and the girl can't train them, either.)

Inversion also takes place when **neither** or **nor** is used as a conjunction to introduce a second clause (see 1.4.7).

1.4.4 Negative questions

Good heavens! **Aren't you** in London this week?
Didn't you buy tickets for the London Opera some time ago?
Phew! **Isn't** it hot in here?

In spoken English, the word **not** is normally contracted to **n't**, and attached to the auxiliary verb. There is always an element of surprise or bewilderment in negative questions, and they are often exclamations. The speaker had previously assumed the fact which he or she now questions:
Aren't you in London? (I thought you were there.)

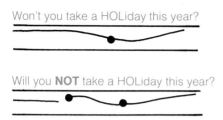

Won't you take a HOLiday this year?

Will you **NOT** take a HOLiday this year?

In negative questions, the intonation tune normally rises after the syllable bearing the principal stress.

If we want to stress the word **not**, we do not contract it, and we place it immediately after the subject. This does not happen often in everyday conversation.
(For negative imperatives, see 1.3.)

1.4.5 Special words in questions and negatives

Customer	Shopkeeper
I'd like **some** peaches.	– Sorry, there are**n't any** peaches left.
I wanted **some** grapes, **too**.	– Sorry, we have**n't any** of those, **either**. We've got **a lot** of nice apples, you know.
– No, thanks. I've already bought **some** apples.	
What about bananas?	– They're **not** in season **yet**.
There isn't **much** fruit at this time of year, is there?	– Oh, I don't know. There are **still** five or six different kinds you can buy.

You have to be careful when you use certain English expressions: **a lot**, **already**, **some**, **still**, **too**, belong mainly in affirmative statements; **any**, **much**, **either**, **yet**, belong mainly in negative statements or in questions.

1.4.6 Answers and responses

In conversation there is a need for all sorts of short answers and expressions, with which we can give small items of information, or express our agreement, our disagreement, our doubts, or simply show that we are paying attention.

What's your name, please?	– **Jack McLean**.
What nationality?	– **British**.
How old are you?	– **Eighteen**.

Answers to **Wh**-questions (**What**? **When**? **Where**? **How**? etc.) may consist of just the fact that is required.

Will you come with me?	– **Certainly**./**OK**.
And you are from Scotland?	– **Yes**.
Do you like travelling?	– **Naturally**.
Have you been to France?	– **No, not yet**./**Never**.
Are you hungry?	– **Of course**! We haven't eaten since seven o'clock.
You won't eat all the biscuits, will you?	– **Of course not**! I'm not a pig.

We use expressions like **Certainly**, **OK**, **Yes**, **Of course**, on their own to express agreement, willingness or to give an affirmative answer.

We use expressions like **No**, **Never**, **Not yet**, **Of course not**, to express disagreement, unwillingness, or to give a negative answer.

Can you speak Russian?	– No, I **can't**
Would you like to learn it?	– Yes, I **would**, certainly.
You like languages, **don't** you?	– I **do**, very much.
Your friend **is** better at maths.	– He **is**, I think.
You**'ve got** a camera, I suppose?	– Yes, I **have**.

By including the auxiliary verb (or appropriate part of **be**, **do** or **have**) in a short answer, we can avoid sounding impatient or bad-tempered. Also, if we include the auxiliary, the answer often sounds more emphatic. But even the shortest answers, **Yes** and **No**, sound friendly enough, if they are said with a rising intonation tune.

NOTES

In your own language, the answer to the question Do you like oranges? may translate as 'Yes, I like.' Note that in English this way of answering is not possible. Correct answers to Do you like oranges? in English are Yes, I do./No, I don't. Similarly, the answer to Do you want to come? is Yes, I do/No, I don't.

1.4.7 *So/too; Neither/Nor/either*

My sister hates spinach.	– **So does** mine. (Mine does, **too**.)
But I **can** eat it.	– **So can** I. (I can, **too**.)
She **is** fond of carrots.	– **So is** my sister. (My sister is, **too**.)

So (at the beginning of a sentence) and **too** (at the end) are used to make short responses which depend for their meaning on the previous speaker's remark. We can regard them as providing additional parallel information. These responses repeat any auxiliary used in the previous speaker's sentence, but if there is none, substitute the appropriate form of **do**, as in other sentences where inversion takes place.

It's raining again!	– **So** it is!
We'll be there in a few minutes now.	{ – **So** we shall! { – Yes, we will.

Bill plays the piano.

– He plays the violin, **too**.
– He plays the violin, **also**.
– He **also** plays the violin.

Tom drinks a lot of wine.

– **AND** beer!
(= He drinks a lot of beer, **too**!
   He **also** drinks a lot of beer!)

NOTES

a) **Also** and **too** are similar in meaning, but we can place **also** either in front of or after the words it refers to, without changing the meaning. If we want to express the same meaning as the two examples with **also**, **too** has come at the end of the sentence.

b) A heavily stressed **AND** at the beginning of a response can mean the same as **too** or **also**.

	Aux + S
Bill was never punctual.	– **Neither** was Joan.
He couldn't get up in time.	– **Nor** could she.

Negative responses are made with **Neither** or **Nor** instead of **so**. Notice the inversion once again.

	S + Aux
Jack can't speak French.	– Mary can't, **either**.
So he never went to France.	– She didn't, **either**.

And in negative responses **either** replaces **too.** Here we use the normal word order.

He doesn't love his wife.	– **NOR** his children!

The negative equivalent of stressed **AND** is **NOR**.

1.4.8 Opinions (... *so*)

	Positive opinion	Negative opinion
Are your friends coming today?	– I think so.	– I don't think so.
Will they bring their their records?	– I suppose so.	– I don't suppose so.
That means a lot of noise.	– I'm afraid so.	– I'm afraid not.
But your neighbours are away?	– I hope so.	– I hope not.

Verbs which express an opinion (**think so, hope so, suppose so, be afraid so, imagine so**), are used in a construction where **so** = what you have just said or asked. (e.g. Are your friends coming today? – I don't think so. = I don't think my friends are coming today.)

1.5 Exclamations

What/How	Complement/O/Adj	S	V
'What	an interesting GRAMmar	this	is!
'What	a nice HOLiday	we	had!
'How	WARM	it	was!
'What	a lot of STRAWberries	(there	were)!
'Wasn't it	MARvellous!		

In exclamations we place **What** + *complement/object* or **How** + *adjective* at the beginning of the sentence, and *S + V* then follow. If subject and verb are obvious from the context, we may leave them out. *Negative questions* may also be used as exclamations (see 1.4.4).

The intonation tune is always the same: the voice starts high, falls on the nuclear stress (noun or adjective), and then remains low.

2 The complex sentence

In English there are many possible ways of joining simple sentences together. We shall explain the most important of these in this section, with notes on their peculiarities and functions. It will be necessary to use the following terms: *complex sentences*, *clause*, *main clause*, *dependent clause*, *conjunction*.

2.1 Sentence connection with *and, or, but*

Main clause	Conj	Main clause
Peter speaks French	**and**	Mary speaks Spanish.
So they can travel to France	**or**	they can go to Spain.
My friends like their French teacher	**but**	they hate learning French.

The conjunctions **and**, **or**, **but** join main clauses, i.e. clauses which are of equal rank or importance.

2.2 Use of *and, or, but*

Peter **knows** French and **he knows** Spanish, too.
Peter knows French and Spanish.
So he could travel to France or Spain.

Mary **speaks** English, but **she** doesn't **speak** Russian.
Mary speaks English, but not Russian.

To avoid repeating words unnecessarily after **and**, **or**, **but**, we may leave out of the second clause any words which we have already said in the first clause, and so we end up with one clause instead of two.

Bill was READing and Jane was playing PING-pong.

The first clause is often said with a rising intonation tune. In this way the speaker signals that there is a second clause to come. Conversely, a falling intonation tune signals that a particular statement is complete.

Mary can 'sing and DANCE.

When words are left out of the second clause, there is usually only one stress. The first clause loses its stress.

Tea is NICE but coffee is HORrible.

The main clause before **but** is said with falling-rising intonation. This signals to us that we should expect a qualification or objection in the second main clause which follows **but**.

2.3 Main clause and dependent clause

Dependent clauses may be built into main clauses in various ways. Sections 2.3.1 to 2.3.14 will deal with each of these ways in turn. For convenience, we shall also deal with relative clauses and adverbial clauses in this section.

2.3.1 Relative clauses

The commonest use of relative clauses is to narrow down the meanings of nouns and make them more specific. (In the examples, **the people who had been invited** is more specific than just **the people**, and **the cake which was left over** is more specific than just **the cake**.) We call this kind of relative clause a *restrictive relative clause* because it narrows down or restricts. The information used to make this restriction is known from, or implied by, the preceding context.

Restrictive

a)

> Three of the people **that/who had been invited** didn't come.
> So the children ate the cake **that/which was left over**.

Punctuation: *Restrictive relative clauses* are not marked off from the main clause by commas.

a) The correct choice of relative pronoun depends on the noun to which it refers: **who** or **that** for persons, **which** or **that** for animals or things.

b)

> The boy **whose** bicycle was stolen went to the police.
> The dog **whose** master had been killed died itself within a week.
> The police moved the car **whose** lights were broken to a garage.

b) The pronoun **whose** can refer to all kinds of noun.

c)

> England has **the best** tea **that** one can buy.
> **Everything** else **that** we tried tasted worse.
> The **only** exception **that** came near the English quality was tea in Australia.
> However, **most** coffee **that** you can get in England is poor stuff.
> I still haven't found **any that** is really drinkable.

c) The relative pronoun **that** is normal after indefinite pronouns (e.g. **all**, **any**, **anything**, **everything**, **most**, **only**) and after superlatives (e.g. **the best**).

d)

| The player | who whom that | they interviewed first did not speak English very well. |

d) There are two forms of the relative pronoun used to refer to persons as objects of the clause: **who** is usual in colloquial spoken English; **whom** is more formal and found mainly in written English (though **who** is found in written English, too). We cannot use **who** after a preposition (see f) below).

e)

The chairman wanted to sell the players **in whom** the manager put all his trust.
He played with skills **of which** other players could only dream.

e) After a preposition we may only use **whom** or **which**, never **who** or **that**.

f)

The chairman wanted to sell the player (**that**) the manager put his trust **in**.
He played with skills (**that**) other players could only dream **of**.

f) But we may also put the preposition at the end of the relative clause, and then we may use **that** instead of **which** or **whom**.

   We may also omit the relative pronoun altogether, if the preposition is at the end.

Non-restrictive

One of the trees, **which** had caught the full force of the wind, had lost several branches.

Another type of relative clause is *non-restrictive*. Only the relative pronouns **who** and **which** (not **that**) may be used in *non-restrictive relative clauses*.

   The information contained in this type of relative clause cannot narrow down the meanings of nouns, because they are already specific or even unique, but is only an addition to what we already knew.

Punctuation: One comma, or two commas, separate a main clause from a non-restrictive relative clause.

a)

| His only sister, His mother, | **whom** he loved very much, died when he was still in his teens. |

a) Non-restrictive relative clauses are naturally found after nouns which cannot be restricted in any way.

b)

> She was always late, **which** he hated.

b) Non-restrictive relative clauses sometimes refer to the main clause as a whole. On these occasions only the pronoun **which** may be used.

2.3.1.1 Reducing relative clauses

The book $\left\{\begin{array}{l}\textbf{which} \text{ he bought} \\ \textbf{that} \text{ he bought}\end{array}\right\}$ was a real best seller.

The girl $\left\{\begin{array}{l}\textbf{whom} \text{ he wanted to marry} \\ \textbf{that} \text{ he wanted to marry}\end{array}\right\}$ disappeared.

The firm **in which** he had worked all his life closed down.

The firm – he had worked **in** all his life closed down.

The relative pronoun may be left out of a restrictive relative clause, if it is not the subject of the clause. When it is part of a prepositional phrase, the relative pronoun may be left out only if the preposition is not the first word of the relative clause.

The relative pronoun cannot be left out of a non-restrictive relative clause.

Father: 'What happened to that shockproof, waterproof, unbreakable, antimagnetic watch I gave you for your birthday?'

Son: 'I lost it!'

Cars $\left\{\begin{array}{l}\textbf{which have} \\ \textbf{with}\end{array}\right\}$ five gears are more economical.

Children $\left\{\begin{array}{l}\textbf{who have no} \\ \textbf{without}\end{array}\right\}$ brothers and sisters may be self-centred.

The man $\left\{\begin{array}{l}\textbf{who lives} \\ \textbf{living}\end{array}\right\}$ next door is a foreigner.

By using various tricks of style we can avoid using some restrictive clauses altogether.

> His father, a famous musician, rarely came home.

Some non-restrictive clauses can be replaced with simple *apposition*; that is, simply placing one noun or noun phrase next to another, with a comma between them.

2.3.1.2 Intonation of relative clauses

'People who 'drive shouldn't DRINK.

If a restrictive relative clause is reasonably short, it is built into the intonation tune of the main clause.

His FAther, who was a 'famous muSIcian, 'rarely came HOME.

A non-restrictive relative clause is given an intonation tune separate from that of the main clause. It is often marked off from the main clause by pauses at beginning and end, corresponding to the commas when we write it down.

2.3.2 Noun clauses as subjects and objects

S-clause				V	O/Adj, etc.
What	he	saw	surprised		him.
Conj	S	V			

A noun clause may serve as either the subject or the object of a main clause. The order of the parts in the dependent clause is the same as in the main clause: $S – V – O$.

S-clause				V	O/Adj, etc.
That	a dog	could play	poker	was	news to him.
Conj	S	Aux + V	O		

The noun clause is made dependent on the main clause by a conjunction, e.g. **what** or **that**, which is the first word in the clause.

S	V	O-clause		
He	knew	that the journey	was	expensive.
But he	hoped	that he	would be able	to save some money.
		S	V	Adj/O

The noun clause may precede the main clause on which it depends, or follow it.

2.3.3 Adverbial clauses

After he had visited his aunt he went to his parents.
He had not seen his family **since** he left the village.
When he came home there was a big party.
In fact, **whenever** he returned there was a party.

Jack **will telephone** you as soon as he **gets** to London.
He **will see** you immediately when he **returns**.

You **will** have to walk because there **won't** be a bus.

You may camp **wherever** you like.
But pitch the tents **where** the ground is flat.
Where the ground is sandy, tents won't stay up.

Please turn off the radio, **because** the baby is asleep.
Since you have a room of your own, you can listen there.
Don't touch that pot, **as** it's very hot.

We went indoors because it was freezing. = We went indoors
   because of the cold.

I'm going to evening classes (**in order**) **to** study accounting.
We climbed onto the wall **so as to** get a better view.

We took a taxi **so that** we wouldn't get wet.
I'll sit here **so (that)** nobody need move if I have to get up and
   answer the phone.

Adverbial clauses of time are introduced by conjunctions such as **after**, **as soon as**, **before**, **since**, **till**, **until**, **when**. We can put these adverbial clauses in front of or after main clauses.

NOTES

a) The following rule applies only to *time clauses* and *conditional clauses*. If both the main clause and the dependent adverbial clause refer to the future, only the main clause has a verb in the future tense.

b) This rule does not necessarily apply to clauses which, for example, give a reason.

Adverbial clauses of place are introduced by **where** or **wherever**. These, too, can come before or after the main clause.

Adverbial clauses of reason are introduced by **as**, **because**, **since**. Again, they can come before or after the main clause.

Note that sometimes we can replace **because** + clause with **because of** + noun phrase.

Adverbial clauses of purpose: Purpose is very commonly expressed by **to**, **in order to**, or **so as to**, followed by an infinitive.

   In order to is more formal than **to** on its own, and therefore less common in conversational English.

A clause introduced by **so that** or **in order that** also expresses purpose. The verb in the clause of purpose is then often **can**, **could**, **will**, **would** or **needn't**. In conversation, **so that** is sometimes shortened to **so**.

Adverbial clauses of purpose may come before or after the main clause.

What are you sitting in the dark **for**? – **To** rest my eyes.

Questions with **What ... for**? ask about purpose or reason.

She was my best friend, **so** I miss her.
There was a power-cut, **and so** we all went to bed.
I think John's letter is rude, **therefore** I shall ignore it.
Prices have risen steeply this year, **and** workers are **therefore** demanding a rise in wages.

Adverbial clauses of result very commonly begin with **so** or **and so**. **Therefore** also shows result, and may be used at the beginning, in the middle, or at the end of a clause. If **therefore** is not the first word in the clause, we have to use **and** as well.

I'm **so** hungry **(that)** I could eat a horse.
They ate **so** quickly they got stomachache.
We ate **so much** food **(that)** we nearly burst.
He told **so many** lies **that** we called him Billy Liar.

So also combines with adjectives and adverbs to show result. To achieve the same meaning we can also use **so much** or **so many**, either on their own, or with a following noun.

He told **such a** (tall) story **(that)** no one believed him. **(Also:** He told **such** tall stories ...)
It was **such a** hot day **(that)** the roads began to melt.

Similarly, **such a** combines with *Adj + noun singular* or a singular noun on its own. Both expressions are followed optionally by **that**.

He hated venison, **although** he was a hunter, **whereas** his wife was quite fond of it.

Adverbial clauses of contrast are introduced by **although, though, whereas, while**, and like other adverbial clauses, may come before or after the main clause.

Always start the engine **as** the manual tells you.
He rides a horse **as if** he were made of wood.
Please read the poem **(in) the way** I shall now demonstrate.

Adverbial clauses of manner are introduced by **as, as if**, or **(in) the way**. As a rule these adverbial clauses follow their main clauses.

Overview of the most useful conjunctions	Type of adverbial clause
after, as soon as, before, since, when, whenever, while, until/till	Time
where, wherever	Place
as, because, since	Reason
in order that, so that	Purpose
so, and so, therefore, so + Adj/Adv + **that, such**	Result
although/though, whereas, while	Contrast
as, as if, (in) the way	Manner

NOTES

a) **In order that** is rather formal; **so that** is more colloquial.

b) **Though** (but not **although**) may also be put at the end of a main cause, e.g. We grew up in the same village. I don't know him very well, **though**. (There is no difference between this and Though we grew up in the same village, I don't know him very well. except that we write it as two separate sentences instead of one complex one, i.e. the difference is purely formal.)

2.3.4 Clauses of comparison

A computer can work **faster than** a human being (can).
It also makes **fewer** mistakes **than** a man (does).
But no machine is **as** ingenious **as** the human brain (is).
It is not even **so/as** clever **as** some animals (are).
A computer has **more** keys **than** a typewriter.
But a typewriter costs **less** money **than** a computer.
Working with a computer is **more/less** interesting than working with a typewriter.

Clauses of comparison follow main clauses which contain one of the following features (see 4.3.6):
Adj + **er than**
more Adj/Adv **than**
less Adj/Adv **than**
as Adj/Adv **as**
not so/as Adj/Adv **as**
more N **than**
fewer countable N **than**
less uncountable N **than**

2.3.5 Use of comparison

In clauses of comparison, the auxiliary verb from the main clause (or the appropriate form of **do**) may either be repeated or left out, as you wish. If it is left out, the style is more colloquial; if it is kept in, more formal.

If the clause of comparison contains entirely different words from the main clause, nothing may be left out. (See, for example, the cartoon opposite.)

'I won't go into details – I've already told you more than I heard myself.'

My father is still bigger { than **I am/he is/she is,** etc.
than **me/him/her,** etc.

If the verb is left out, use **me, him,** etc. not **I, he; than I** sounds very pedantic nowadays.

Wales is **not** { so large as } Scotland.
as large as }

In negative comparisons, **so ... as** and **as ... as** have exactly the same meaning.

2.3.6 Conditional clauses

If it rains we'**ll stay** at home.
But we **shall go** to the zoo **if** the weather **is** fine.
So **be ready in time if** you **want** to come.
If you **have promised** to come, you **must come.**

Conditional clauses are introduced by **if.** They may come before or after the main clause.

The condition is considered to be a *real condition* (i.e. a real possibility) if the verb in the **if**-clause is in any of the following tenses: present simple, present continuous, or present perfect; and if the verb in the main clause is in the present or future tense or is an imperative.

If I **was/were** you I **would learn** English and French.
And then, if I **had** a one-year holiday, I'**d travel** through Europe.
I **wouldn't waste** a minute if I **were** given the chance.

But the condition is considered to be improbable or hypothetical (an *unreal* or *impossible condition*) if the **if**-clause contains a verb in *past tense*, and the main clause has **would/'d** (sometimes also **could, might**) + *base form* of a verb. When **if**-clauses express unreal conditions, the form of **be** may be **were** in all persons, though **was** is also used for singular persons in colloquial English.

If Peter **hadn't parked** his car there, the police **wouldn't have towed** it away.

If we are imagining that the *unreal condition* (or possibility) existed in the past, the verb in the **if**-clause is in past perfect tense, and the main clause contains **would/wouldn't** + present perfect, or sometimes **could/ couldn't, might/mightn't** or **should/ shouldn't** instead of **would/ wouldn't.**

> **Unless** you work hard, you won't pass the exam.
> And you'll have to pass it, **unless** you want to leave school.

a) **Unless** is the negative counterpart of **if** and obeys the same rules. But we can't use it if we are imagining the past to be different from what it really was, e.g. in If I hadn't turned off the electricity, he would have been killed we can't substitute **unless I had** for **if I hadn't**.

> If prices **rise,** demand **falls.**
> But if prices **fall,** demand usually **grows.**

b) We can only use *present simple* in both **if**-clause and main clause if the two clauses together express a natural law or an invariable result.

> If you **would** all please **listen** very carefully, I **will** now **tell** everyone the date of his or her next appointment.

c) Use of **would** in the **if**-clause instead of **will** is a very polite way of showing that we think or hope a condition will be (or can be) fulfilled.

2.3.7 Direct and indirect speech

> William: 'I've lost my dog.'
> Mary: 'Are you going to put a notice in the paper?'
> William: 'Don't be silly. He can't read.'

In *direct speech* we quote the actual words a speaker said. The words are marked off at either end with quotation marks. (Note that in English, quotation marks are like this: "_____" or this: '_____'.)

> Jack is on the phone. He **says that** he'd like to take you out for dinner.
> He also **says that** he'll pick you up about 8 o'clock.

In *indirect speech* one speaker's words are reported by someone else. We make it clear this is happening by using in the main clause a verb such as **reply, say, tell, ask, answer,** etc. The indirect speech is contained in a dependent clause.

In indirect speech, the main clause may precede the dependent clause, or follow it. The conjunction **that** may be left out if the order is *main clause + dependent clause* (see (a) opposite). It *must* be left out if the order is *dependent clause + main clause* (see (b) opposite).

a) He says (that) he'll pick you up.
b) Jack is on the phone. He'll pick you up at 8 o'clock he says.

2.3.8 Backshift of tenses

Suppose you are making a report, giving an account as a witness, or simply passing on a message. You may find yourself in the position of having to convert direct speech into indirect speech. You will then need to pay close attention to the tense of the verb in the main clause, on which the reported speech clause depends.

Little John:	'I want to play with the dog.'	→ Little John says that he wants to play with the dog.

If the verb with a meaning like **say**, in the main clause, is in *present tense* (or even *present perfect* or *future*), the tenses in the dependent clause are the same for both direct speech and indirect speech.

William:	'I've lost my dog.'	→ William says that he has lost his dog.

If, however, the verb with a meaning like **say** is in *past tense*, there are the following differences between direct and indirect speech:

1.	Bill:	'I **am** very hungry.'	→ Bill **said** that he **was** very hungry;
2.		'I **haven't eaten** for hours.'	that he **hadn't eaten** for hours,
3.		'And I **had** breakfast at 6 o'clock in the morning!'	and that he **had had** breakfast at 6 o'clock in the morning.
4.		'But I **will** not **have** a large meal.'	But he **would** not **have** a large meal, he said.

Direct speech	Indirect speech
1. Present	→Past
2. Present perfect Past perfect	}→Past perfect
3. Past	→Past or past perfect*
4. **will**-future (including **shall**)	→**would**

* If the time sequence is clear, it is not essential to backshift the past tense in indirect speech.

Legless, ...
An artificial leg in the lost property department at Bristol Police H.Q. has been claimed by a Scotsman who said he had been drinking.

Bill said,
'We are planning our holidays.' → Bill said that they **were**
planning their holidays.

'It **cannot** be done.' → They said it **couldn't** be done.
'I **may** be late.' → She said she **might** be late.
'You **shall** see it soon.' → He said they **should** see it soon.
'There **will** be a disaster soon.' → People said that there **would** be
a disaster soon.
'Your friend **must** leave.' → He said that my friend **must**
leave/**had to** leave.
'We **oughtn't to** stay long.' → She said they **oughtn't to/didn't**
ought to stay long.

'**I wish** that I **was/were** ten years younger.'
He says he **wishes** he **was/were** ten years younger.

Copernicus **said** that all planets **move** round the sun.

NOTES

a) If direct speech uses a continuous tense, the verb in indirect speech should also be continuous.

b) Most auxiliaries change form when backshift occurs. The changes are as follows:

Direct speech	Indirect speech
can	→**could**
may	→**might**
shall	→**should**
will	→**would**

The auxiliaries **must** and **ought to** are the same in direct and indirect speech, as they have no past tense forms (though in the negative, **didn't ought to** in indirect speech may replace **oughtn't to** in direct speech).

In indirect speech, **had to/hadn't to** is often used to replace **must/mustn't** in direct speech, because then we can make the normal tense change after **said**, etc.

(For the substitute forms of auxiliaries in other tenses, see 3.7.)

c) Because of the uncertainty whether wishes can ever be fulfilled, all wishes introduced by the verb **wish** are always expressed in past tense, even though they refer to present time.

Were is an alternative to **was** in this use.

d) Sometimes the rules on backshift are not obeyed. This is so if the statement is a general truth, which applies just as much now as when the statement was originally made.

2.3.9 Change of pronouns and adverbials

Bill: 'I like rock music.'	→ Bill said he liked rock music.
Mary and Joan: 'We prefer jazz.'	→ Mary and Joan said that they preferred jazz.
Peter to Anne: 'You dance very well.'	→ (Anne reporting): Peter said that I could dance very well.

When you are choosing *pronouns* in indirect speech you must ask yourself: Who is reporting about whom? To take as an example the last sentence opposite, if Mark had been reporting, not Anne, it would have been: Peter said that she (=Anne) could dance very well.

Adverbials of time have to be chosen with care, in order to keep the time reference of direct speech and indirect speech the same:

a)

John: 'I haven't seen Julia **today**.'	→ John says (that) he hasn't seen Julia **today**.
'I asked her **yesterday**.'	→ He says he asked her **yesterday**.
'We'll go to a disco **tomorrow**.'	→ They will go to a disco **tomorrow**.

a) Reporting on the same day when the direct speech occurred.

b)

	→ John said that he hadn't seen Julia **that day**.
	→ He said he had asked her **the day before**.
	→ They would go to a disco **the next/the following day**.

b) Reporting one or more days after the direct speech occurred.

Using these time expressions avoids any possible confusion between the time when the direct speech took place and the time when it is being reported.

Adverbials of place also need care. We have to think about the location of the speaker at the time the direct speech occurred, in relation to that of the reporter at the time the indirect speech occurs:

a)

| Ruth: | 'I lost the money **here**.' | → Ruth said she had lost her money **here**. |

'I'm certain it is some-where **in this room**.' → She was certain it was somewhere **in this room**.

b) → Ruth said she had lost her money **there**.
→ She was certain it was somewhere **in that room**.

a) The reporter is still in the same location

b) The reporter is now somewhere else.

Here, this, these always refer to the speaker's present location, or something in it; whilst **there, that, those** refer to some other place or something in it (see *demonstrative pronouns* 4.5.6).

2.3.10 Indirect questions

| Peter: | 'Can I help you, Mary?' | → Peter **asked** Mary **whether/if** he could help her. |
| Mary: | 'Did you see my watch anywhere?' | → Mary **wondered whether/if** he had seen her watch. |

It **depends on** whether we are punctual.

| Jill: | '**When** is Tom's birthday?' | → Jill wanted to know **when** Tom's birthday was. |
| Jack: | '**Why** do you want to know?' | → Jack wondered **why** she wanted to know. |

For **Yes/No** questions, the verb in the main clause will be **ask, wonder, enquire,** etc. or an expression such as **want to know**. The *main clause* is connected to the *dependent clause* (= the indirect question) by **if** or **whether**.

Note that after a phrasal verb, we can use **whether** but not **if**.

With **Wh**-questions the **Wh**-word of the direct question is used to begin the dependent clause of the corresponding indirect question. The order in the dependent clause is always: **Wh**-*word* (= conjunction) – *S – Aux – V*, etc., that is, the order of a main clause.

2.3.11 Indirect imperatives

a)
Tom **told/asked** her to go to the station immediately.
The police **advised/recommended** me not to tell anyone what I had seen.

a) In the commonest type of indirect imperative, an *infinitive clause* is generally preferred as the dependent clause to a clause with a finite verb (see 2.3.12). But note that only some verbs can be used in this way. They include **advise, ask, instruct, order, recommend, tell,** but not **demand, propose, suggest.**

b)

| Tom to Mary: | 'Don't forget your ticket.' | → | Tom **told** Mary that she **shouldn't** forget her ticket. |
| | 'Go to the station immediately.' | → | He **demanded** that she **should** go to the station immediately. |

b) Alternatively, the verbs listed under (a) may be used with the conjunction **that**. The verb in the dependent clause always consists of **shall** or **should** (with or without negative) + the *base form* of a verb (see 2.3.12). The usual rules of tense back-shift (**shall** → **should**) apply, and so do changes of pronouns and adverbials (see 2.3.9). But avoid using **ask** with **that**, as it often sounds unnatural.

c)

| Tom | suggested proposed recommended | that she should go to the station immediately. |

c) Imperatives are often softened, so that we might equally well regard them as requests or even suggestions (see 5.5). In indirect speech this is reflected in the choice of verb used in the main clause.

2.3.12 Infinitive clauses

We frequently use infinitive clauses to shorten and simplify clauses of the *S + V + O* type. Moreover, there are certain verbs, adjectives and nouns which require infinitive clauses after them. These will be dealt with separately.

His only aim was **to win** the race.

Present infinitive, active: **to** + *base form* of the verb.

NOTES
Other forms:

To have worked hard all those years for nothing was a huge disappointment.

Perfect infinitive, active voice: **to** + **have** + *past participle*

Not **to be mentioned** in the honours list didn't worry him.

Present infinitive, passive voice: **to** + **be** + *past participle*

But **to have been forgotten** by his own colleagues upset him terribly.

Perfect infinitive, passive voice: **to** + **have been** + *past participle*

Peter was the one man { who could help us. / **to help** us.

Do you have anyone { who you could talk to? / **to talk** to?

Many *restrictive relative clauses* can be shortened to *infinitive clauses*.

That he had been forgotten again / **To have been forgotten** again } made him angry.

I hope { that I'll see you next Tuesday. / **to see** you next Tuesday.

A *subject clause* can be shortened to an *infinitive clause*, if the main clause and the dependent clause of the sentence both have the same subject (or object, as the case may be). (In the first example, **he** = **him**; in the second, **I** = **I**.)

With certain verbs (especially **agree, demand, expect, hope, pretend,** an *object clause* can also be shortened, again providing the subjects of both clauses are the same.

Clauses beginning with **Wh-***pronouns* may also be shortened, if two conditions are fulfilled
– they must refer to a future happening or possibility;
– the subjects of main clause and dependent clause must be the same.

'Don't ask me. I've only just learned how to spell cat.'

a)

Jack didn't know { where he should go. / where **to go.**

He wondered { when he should phone his parents. / when to phone his parents.

He tried to remember { how one used an American telephone. / how to use an American telephone.

This applies to both
a) **Wh-***clauses* which function as objects; and

b)

Mary asked her instructor { what she could do if the engine stopped. / what **to do** if the engine stopped.

She wondered { how she might help the hungry people of Africa. / how **to help** the hungry people of Africa.

b) *indirect questions.*

Bill told Jane
{ that she should not forget her umbrella.
{ not **to forget** her umbrella.
He also asked her **to buy** the tickets.

Indirect imperatives are very often shortened to infinitive clauses if the verb is **tell,** etc., and almost always if the verb is **ask** (see 2.3.12 (b)).

'*But if I don't wait for him to phone,
how can I tell him to get lost?*'

She **warned** him **to be** careful.
She **warned** him **not to close** the door.
She **wanted** him **to talk** to her sister.

As a rule **warn** is followed by O_d + **(not) to** + *infinitive.*

After **want** (and its negative forms **don't want, didn't want,** etc.) we always have **to** + *infinitive*, never a finite dependent clause.

The wall was **too strong to be pulled down.**
But it wasn't **high enough to keep** dogs out.

We also use infinitives after **too** + *Adj* or *Adj* + **enough.**

John wanted **his sister to join** the team.
He believed **her to be** a good tennis player.
The team expected **the newcomer to improve** their chances of winning the championship.
They forced her **to practise** several hours each day.

The teacher **made them copy** the text.
The teacher **let them copy** the text.

It is sometimes possible for the infinitive to have its own subject. This happens with *indirect imperatives* (see 2.3.11). It also occurs with a number of verbs, such as **believe, cause, expect, force, help, want, let, make.**

Notice that **let** and **make** are different from the other verbs, as they are followed by *infinitive without* **to.**

'Somehow I expected your half-
brother to be smaller . . .'

> The dog **waited for** his master **to come out.**
> The children **were longing for** their parents **to come back.**
> They **counted on** the policeman **to help them**.
> They had an address **for him to check**.
> It was difficult **for him to find.**

NOTES
We also find infinitives with their own subjects after various verbs, nouns and adjectives which have adverbial particles or prepositions attached to them.

2.3.13 Participial clauses

A *participial clause* (= clause beginning with a *verb base* + ***ing***) is often used to shorten and simplify a dependent clause, in much the same way that an infinitive clause does. In addition, there are certain verbs which are typically followed by participial clauses.

> He came in, **looking** rather pleased with himself.
> **Having cleaned** the car, he needed a rest.
> **Having been blamed** for something he hadn't done, he went to his room and sulked.
> He felt embarrassed, **being paid** for doing nothing.

Use of the *perfect participle* (= ***having*** + *past participle*) shows that the participial clause happened before the main clause; but use of the *present participle* (= *verb base* + ***ing*** only) shows that two clauses happened at the same time. Sometimes a participial clause may sound like a *cause* or *reason*, e.g. Having cleaned the car he needed a rest = Because he had cleaned the car, he needed a rest. In the passive, the *present participle* consists of ***being*** + *past participle* and the *perfect participle* of ***having been*** + *past participle*. The subjects of main clause and dependent participial clause have to be the same. The participial clause may come before or after the main clause.

43

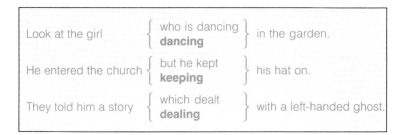

Look at the girl	who is dancing / **dancing**	in the garden.
He entered the church	but he kept / **keeping**	his hat on.
They told him a story	which dealt / **dealing**	with a left-handed ghost.

Relative clauses and *adverbial clauses of time* may be made shorter by using *present participles*.

Sheila **came running,** as soon as she was called, but Jack **left** all his
    books **lying** about, and **kept** everybody **waiting.**
So they **sent** him **shopping.**
Don't **go crying** to your mother!

The most common verbs which may be followed by present participles are **come, go, keep (on), leave, remain, send.**

| Neighbours saw him | **crossing** / **cross** | the street. |
| They heard him | **singing** / **sing** | a song. |

NOTES

a) Verbs of perception, such as **hear, see, watch,** may be followed by either an *infinitive without to,* or by a *present participle.* Use of the infinitive emphasizes that the whole of the action was observed; but use of the participle suggests that only part of a continuous, but incomplete action was observed, and then something else happened. For example, if we add the words 'and then he fell dead' to 'Neighbours saw him cross the street', we understand that he died on the pavement on the far side of the road. But if we add the same words to 'Neighbours saw him crossing the street'. we understand he died on the street.

b) In 1.1.2 and 1.1.3.1 we saw that we can also use *base form* of the verb + **ing** as a noun subject or noun object.

It's **no use crying** over spilt milk.
It's **worth visiting** the British Museum.
The British Museum is **worth visiting.**

Base form of the verb + **ing** also follows the expressions **It's no use, It's worth,** and **N is worth.**

After he had learnt
After **having learnt**
After **learning** } French he went to Paris.
    Having learnt

Adverbial clauses of time are often shortened by use of participles. If the conjunction **after** is left out, we can only understand the precise meaning of the shortened dependent clause from its context. The third and fourth examples are the ones we hear most often in everyday speech.

As she   **had been told**
    Having been told } to leave, she went at once.
         Told

People { who **are hurt** } in a game can claim money from
        {   **hurt** } . the club's insurance company.

Some clauses in the passive may be reduced to the perfect participle or even the past participle only.

Mary **had** her hair **cut,** and **got** her bicycle **repaired.**

NOTES
Have/get something done means 'employ someone to do something for you'. Contrast Mary **had cut** her hair. = She had cut it herself.

2.3.14 Special emphasis

The butter he had forgotten, but not the bread.
The book he gave to Mary, and the paper to Joan.
ANgry she WAS but not FURious.

Any departure from normal word order signals special emphasis. The word or words which are taken out of their normal position are stressed heavily in the intonation tune.

It **is** my CAR **that** they damaged.
It **was** the WINdow **that** was broken (not the DOOR).

We can use the expression **It is/It was ... that** to draw attention to a particular part of a sentence. This construction is known as a *cleft sentence.*

    Once again, the intonation tune reflects the importance we want to give to the chosen word or words.

THE PARTS OF THE SENTENCE

3 The verb phrase

3.1 Main verbs

3.1.1 Forms and functions of main verbs

English main verbs have a small number of forms, but a large number of functions. We can derive all the forms of regular verbs from their *base*.

Form	Function
base	– present infinitive, active voice
	– all forms of the present simple tense, except 3rd person singular
s form	– 3rd person singular, present simple tense
ing form	– present participle
	– nouns
ed form	– past simple tense of regular verbs.
	– past participle of regular verbs, used to form perfect tenses and the passive.

Let's **play** table tennis.
We **live** in the same street.

He want**s** to become a doctor.

The cat is sleep**ing** under the car.
Collect**ing** stamps is one of my hobbies.
The cat mew**ed** feebly.
The cat had disappear**ed**.
The cat was sav**ed** by the girl.

Irregular verbs form their past tenses and past participles in a different way, e.g. **write** – **wrote** – **written**. (See Appendix 1, p. 141 for a list.)

3.1.2 Spelling and pronunciation of the verb forms

s form

Spelling	Pronunciation
s all verbs, except the following which end in **es**.	/s/ he sto**ps**, he si**ts**, if the *base* ends in any voiceless consonant (except a sibilant*).
es if the *base* ends in **sh**, **ch**, **s(s)**, **x**, e.g. fini**sh**, wat**ch**, ki**ss**, bo**x**; or if the *base* ends in **y** after a consonant, e.g. hurry, try, when **y** becomes **i**: he hurr**ies**, she tr**ies** but play → play**s**	/z/ he rea**ds**, the child play**s**, if the *base* ends in any voiced consonant* (except a sibilant*), or if it ends in a vowel or a diphthong.
	/ɪz/ School finish**es** at four. Water freez**es** at 0°. This pronunciation applies if the *base* is pronounced with a final sibilant, even if it is written with **e** at the end (e.g. lose → los**es**).

*See p. vi, Phonetic symbols.

She goes	/gəuz/	to work.
He does	/dʌz/	his homework.
He says	/sez/	nothing.

Special spelling and pronunciation forms apply to the verbs **go** /gəʊ/, **do** /duː/ and **say** /seɪ/.

ing form

The following rules apply to the spelling of the **ing** form:

---

s**it** – si**tt**ing, sto**p** – sto**pp**ing
but: eat – eating

gi**ve** – giving, shak**e** – shaking

If there is a single final consonant it is doubled after a vowel written as one letter in a stressed syllable. Silent final **e** is omitted, with very few exceptions, e.g. **ageing, dyeing.**

ed form

Spelling		Pronunciation	
sto**p** – sto**pp**ed	A single final consonant is doubled after a vowel written as one letter in a stressed syllable.	/t/	he stopp**ed**. After any voiceless* consonant (except **t**).
cr**y** – cr**i**ed	**y** after a consonant becomes **i**.	/d/	she clean**ed**, she cri**ed**. After any voiced* consonant (except **d**), and after a vowel or diphthong.
hat**e** – hat**ed**	Silent final **e** is not repeated.	/ɪd/	they hat**ed**, it end**ed**. After **t** or **d**.
sa**y** – sai**d**	An isolated exception.	/seɪ – sed/	

* See p. vi, Phonetic symbols.

NOTES
a) to produce the **ing** and **ed** forms of verbs whose bases end in **r** or **l,** apply the following rules:

final **r** is doubled, if the preceding vowel is in a stressed syllable, and is written as one letter: pre'fe**rr**ed, pre'fe**rr**ing (but 'cove**r**ed, 'cove**r**ing).

final **l** is doubled in BrE (but not in AmE) if the preceding, single letter vowel is unstressed: trave**l** – trave**ll**ed (but appeal – appealed) (AmE: traveled)

b) the **ing** forms of verbs **lie** and **die** are **lying, dying.**

3.1.3 Tense[1] and aspect[2]

By choosing the appropriate form of an English verb we can show not only *when* something happens (= tense), but in many cases also *how* it happens (= aspect).
This is possible because at each tense level there are *two* forms:
– a *simple* form which concentrates on the time of the action or event,
– a *progressive*[3] form (= part of **be** + **ing** form of the verb) which concentrates on the aspect.

[1] Tense: This term is preferred to *time* because *tense* and *time* are not always the same. For example, in English the *present progressive tense* may have either present or future meaning.
[2] Aspect: This term means 'way of looking at something', and indicates that the choice of the form of the verb depends on the viewpoint and attitude of the speaker.
[3] Progressive: Formerly the term *continuous* was widely used to describe these forms, and therefore may be the description employed in a course book you are using.

3.2 Present simple and present progressive

3.2.1 Forms of the present simple

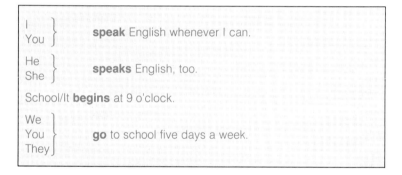

I
You } **speak** English whenever I can.

He
She } **speaks** English, too.

School/It **begins** at 9 o'clock.

We
You } **go** to school five days a week.
They

In *positive statements* the present simple is identical to the *base*, i.e. it has no endings.
   The one exception is the 3rd person singular (**he, she, it** and impersonal **one**), which adds **s** or **es** to the *base* (see 3.1.2).

Do you speak French? – Sorry, I **don't** (speak French).
My friend **doesn't** speak English.

In the present simple, *questions* and *negative statements* are made with the auxiliary **do** (3rd person singular **does**), if no other auxiliary verb is being used (see 1.2.1, 1.4.1).

3.2.2 Forms of the present progressive

Mike and his father	**are**		**watching** TV.
The dog	**is** not		**watching.**
	(= isn't)		
It	**is**		**sleeping.**

The *present progressive* consists of the present tense forms of **be** + *base form* of the verb + **ing.**

What **are** you **doing**? – **Are** you **working**?
No, I **am** not (I'm not) **working** at the moment.

In the present progressive it is the relevant part of the verb **be** which always changes position, or adds **not**, to make questions and negative statements, respectively.

3.2.3 Simple or progressive?

'In my spare time I read or listen to my records. Sometimes I do experiments.'

'Oh John, what are you doing now?'

'Don't worry, Mum. I'm just doing an experiment.'

'We've got holidays now and I'm working at a garage to earn some money for my moped ...'

Uses of *simple tense*:
We use the *present simple* when an action or activity may happen at any time in the present, or when it is not important to state the time.

In the cartoon opposite, the boy wants to tell us what he does generally in his spare time, or whenever there is an opportunity, so he uses *present simple* = the correct tense for talking about hobbies, habits, routines, etc.

Uses of *progressive tense*:
We use the *present progressive* when there is a limit to the duration of the action in time, and especially when something is happening at the actual time of speaking, or over a period of time which includes the present moment.

In the cartoon opposite, the experiment is taking place at the time of the conversation.

In the letter underneath the cartoon, the activity (working at a garage) is not happening at this actual moment (when the boy is in fact writing a letter), but it is happening at various times within a period (a holiday) which includes the present.

49

3.2.4 Use of the present simple

We will now go on from the above comparison of the two tenses, and pick out three major uses of the present simple.

a)

> **I get up** at 7 o'clock every day.
> I (usually) **go** to school by bus.
> What **do** you (normally) **have** for breakfast?

a) We use *present simple* when we want to talk about habits, routines, or any other events or actions which occur either regularly or frequently. With present simple we quite naturally use a number of adverbs which express regularity or frequency, such as **always**, **every** (day, week, year, Sunday, etc), **never**, **normally**, **often**, **sometimes**, **usually**. (This is not to say that these adverbs are used exclusively with *present simple*; they are not.)

b)

> **I pour** this liquid into the test-tube, **mix** it, **heat** it slowly and then . . .

b) We can use *present simple* to describe a series of happenings, e.g. in a report of an experiment, or in a commentary on a sports event, such as a football or tennis match.

c)

> I **think** we're near a village.
> Yes, I can **see** the smoke.
> **Do** you **want** to have a rest there?
> Oh yes, and I **hope** they'll serve us a meal, too.

c) We use *present simple* to express opinions or feelings, e.g. wishes, preferences, likes, and dislikes. Verbs such as **want**, **like**, **hate**, **know**, **remember** and **think** (= believe) are therefore used almost exclusively in simple tense. (For use in *perfect tenses*, see 3.4.2.3.) Statements about things we know about from the use of our senses are often expressed with **can + see/hear**, etc., e.g. I can hear you, but I can't see you.

Note that in English, we don't use present simple to talk about the future, except in certain special circumstances (see 3.6.5).

3.2.5 Use of the present progressive

In addition to the basic rules for the use of present progressive, which we set out in 3.2.3, please note the following important points:

a)

'*What are you thinking about?*'

> Could you call again? We're just **having** lunch.

b)

> What **are** you **looking at**? – That parrot. **Do** you **see** it?
> Why **are**n't you **listening**? – Because I **don't hear** very well.

a) Verbs like **think** and **have** are mostly used as *state verbs* in present simple tense. But as *action verbs** they may also be used in the present progressive. They then tell us about a particular event happening within a limited period.

   When **think** is used as an action verb, it is not usually followed by a dependent clause. Contrast, for example: I think you are right = In my opinion (which is a state of mind).

When **have** is used as an action verb it never has the meaning 'possess' or 'own' (see 3.9.3).

b) Notice the difference between verbs like **look (at)**, **listen (to)**, **watch** and verbs like **see**, **hear**. The first group tell us about things we decide to see or hear (or decide not to see or hear), and they can be used in the progressive form. The second group are concerned with seeing, hearing, etc. when they do not depend on a previous decision, and are normally in simple tense.

*In aspect usage we distinguish between *action verbs* and *state verbs*. Action verbs, such as **come**, **eat**, **go**, **hit**, **sleep**, tell us about actions, activities and events, and occur frequently in progressive tenses. *State verbs*, such as **have** (= 'possess'), **live**, **know**, tell us about states and circumstances, and are normally used in simple tenses only.

3.3 Past simple and past progressive

3.3.1 Forms and use of the past simple

I really **enjoyed** my holiday last summer.
We **travelled** all over England.

And, of course, we **went** to London, too.

Did you **buy** anything in London? –
Well, only a few records. But we **did**n't (= did not) **buy** any souvenirs.

In *positive statements* we form the *past simple* of all regular verbs by adding **ed** to the *base*, in all persons (see 3.1.2).

However, a considerable number of verbs are irregular in their past tense (see Appendix 1).

Questions and *negatives* in past simple are composed of **did** (i.e. the past tense of **do**) + the *base* (see 1.2 and 1.4).

We use the *past simple* when we wish to talk about things which happened in the past and which we regard as being finished with.

'Remember me? Ten years ago you fired me!'

Did you **see** 'Gold Rush' on TV last night? –
No, I **did**n't. I **saw** the film only a few weeks ago.
Charles Spencer ('Charlie') Chaplin was born on April 16, 1889.
At the age of 24 he **went** to the USA. One year later, in 1914, he
   made his first 35 short films.
In London we **saw** Chaplin at the waxworks.

The past simple is concerned with specific events which happened at a certain time in the past, and its principal use is therefore in stories and reports. Specific indications for use of this tense are
– references to time (adverbials like **yesterday**, **last week**, **some time ago**, and years, e.g. **in 1888**).
– contexts which make it clear we are talking about specific events in the past.

3.3.2 Forms and use of the past progressive

> Yesterday I **was watching** TV almost all evening.
> And what **were** YOU **doing,** Tom?

Past progressive	Past simple
We **were having** dinner(,) when suddenly the lights **went out.** When we **were eating,** the telephone **rang.**	

Past progressive	Past progressive
I **was doing** my homework, while my brother **was listening** to his stereo.	

The *past progressive* is made with the appropriate past tense form of **be** (**was** or **were**) + *the **ing** form of the verb.

In contrast to the past simple, the past progressive indicates that a happening in the past continued for some time.

Past progressive and *past simple* are frequently combined, i.e. past progressive appears in one clause of a complex sentence, and past simple in the other. Each tense may appear in either the main clause or the dependent one. There is no obvious difference in the meaning between When we were eating, the telephone rang and We were eating when the telephone rang. We can think of the action in past simple as a punctuation or interruption (temporary or final) of a continuing action, described in past progressive. For example: He was drawing water, when he fell down the well. (An interruption, which presumably ended the action of drawing water!)

We were still running towards the station, when the clock struck one. (A punctuation – if our train was at five past one, we presumably continued running, even faster than before).

The use of *past progressive* in both clauses of a complex sentence emphasizes that both actions were going on at the same time.

NOTES
It is safer to stick to the conjunction **when** in the pattern *past progressive + past simple*; and to the conjunction **while** in the pattern *past progressive + past progressive*.

(1) While we were eating, the bell rang. would have the same meaning as (2) When we were eating, the bell rang. But
(3) We were eating while the bell rang. would mean the same as
(4) We were eating while the bell was ringing.
(1) sounds like a brief interruption by a door bell, but (4) sounds more like the continuous ringing of a church bell.

3.4 Present perfect simple and present perfect progressive

3.4.1 Forms of the present perfect simple

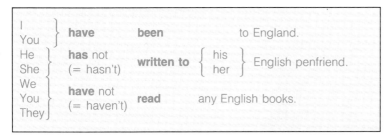

Positive and *negative statements*: The present perfect simple consists of the appropriate present tense form of **have** (**has** or **have**) (with **not** in the negative), followed by the past participle of the verb in question, i.e. *S* + **have** + *past participle*. This past participle may, of course, be either regular or irregular. (See Appendix 1 for irregular past participles.)

Questions: In questions, the appropriate part of **have** (**has** or **have**) changes place with the subject, and the order becomes **have** + *S* + *past participle*.

In statements, no words may come between **have** and the *past participle*, except certain adverbs such as **already**, **always**, **nearly**, **never**, **not yet**, **often**, **still not**.

3.4.2 Use of the present perfect simple

'I have lived on this island for 30 years.'

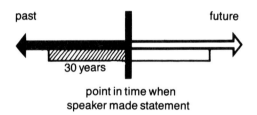

past   **future**

30 years

**point in time when
speaker made statement**

'I lived on that island for about 30 years.'

Use of the *present perfect* makes a connection between the point in time when the statement is made and something which happened in the past. We understand from this that the happening is not finished and done with, but is in some way still relevant to the speaker's present situation. In the cartoon opposite, the man came to the island 30 years ago (an event in the past); but at the time of speaking he is still there, and likely to remain there in the future.

For single events in the past we prefer the *past simple* to the *present perfect* if we want to emphasize that the event is completely restricted to the past and has no relevance to the present situation.

(In the second cartoon, the man has returned to civilization. His long stay of 30 years on the desert island is all in the past. He is not there now, and he is not going back.)

3.4.2.1 Emphasis on result

> I**'ve cleaned** my bike. Look, how clean it is. But someone **has taken** the pump. I can't find it anywhere.

We use the *present perfect simple* to describe actions or happenings in the past, when their result is clear or can be seen at the present time, and is still having an effect.

'Look! I haven't forgotten to bring my umbrella home with me today.'
'But you didn't take it with you!'

> **Have** you (already) **done** the shopping? – Yes, I have.
> – Yes, I've just done it.
> – No, I haven't.
> – No, I haven't done it yet.

The adverbials **already, just, not yet** are often used with verbs in *present perfect* tense. (But please note, they are not used exclusively with this tense.)

3.4.2.2 Present perfect with *ever/never*

> **Have** you **ever been** to Scotland?
> No, I **have never been** there.
> **Have** you **ever seen** the Rolling Stones in concert?
> Oh yes, **I've seen** them several times.
> You know, I'm a Rolling Stones fan.

We use the *present perfect* when we want to talk about activities at any time in a period up to now, without being exact about the time.

If the *present perfect simple* is used in this way, it is often accompanied by the adverbials **ever** (= 'at any time until now') **never** (= 'not at any time until now') or **not yet** (also = 'not until now', but suggesting a greater possibility that the event or activity may happen in the future). But note this does not mean **ever** and **never** are limited to use with the *present perfect*. They are used with other tenses too, e.g. Do you ever go skiing?

	Have you **ever seen** a flying saucer? No, **never.** And I don't think there are such things.
But:	Oh yes, I **saw** one **once.** It **was** in 1979, and I **was** in Canada at the time.

In contrast, this answer is concerned with a particular single event in the past with an exact date, and so the *past simple* is used.

3.4.2.3 Present perfect with *for/since*

In addition to the use described in 3.4.2.2, we also use the *present perfect* when we talk about activities which began in the past and are still continuing at the time of speaking.

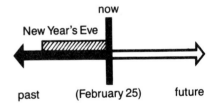

(The couple in the picture met at a dance on New Year's Eve, became friends, and are still friends on February 25th. They expect to remain friends in the future.)

We**'ve known** each other **for** almost two months.
I**'ve** never **thought** I could be in love with someone **for** such a long time.
I**'ve been** in love with you **since** our party on New Year's Eve.
They **have been** sweethearts { **since** New Year's Eve.
{ **for** two months.

The words **for** and **since** are used most often with the *present perfect simple* of the verbs **be**, **have** (= 'possession'), **know** and **see**.

For (with the *present perfect*) introduces a period of time, without directly mentioning the moment in the past when the activity started (**for** 3 days, **for** many years, **for** a long time).

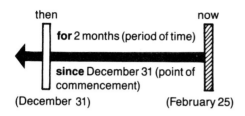

then   now

for 2 months (period of time)

since December 31 (point of commencement)

(December 31)   (February 25)

Since introduces the point when the activity starts, which may be a time (**since** ten o'clock), a date (**since** June, **since** 1980), or an event which happened at a particular time (**since** we first met, **since** I left school).

3.4.3 Forms and use of the present perfect progressive

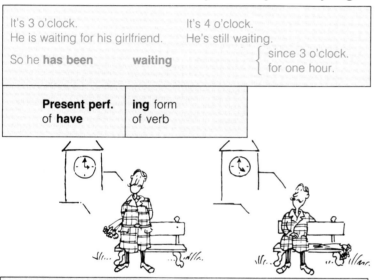

It's 3 o'clock.
He is waiting for his girlfriend.

It's 4 o'clock.
He's still waiting.

So he **has been**   **waiting**
$\begin{cases} \text{since 3 o'clock.} \\ \text{for one hour.} \end{cases}$

Present perf. of **have**	**ing** form of verb

Have you **been waiting** long?
– I**'ve been waiting** all afternoon.
I**'ve been working** as a waiter for 10 years now.
Doctor (to man ill in bed): You**'ve been working** too hard.

Patient: 'I keep thinking I'm a dog.'
Doctor: 'How long **have** you **been feeling** like this?'
Patient: 'Since I was a puppy.'

In questions, the form of **have** is placed before the subject, like an auxiliary (see 1.2).

We use the *progressive* form of the *present perfect* when we are talking about activities or actions which began in the past and are still continuing at the time of speaking, or which have been continuing up to the time of speaking. We are not necessarily doing them at the time of speaking itself, e.g. The man who has been working as a waiter for 10 years may give us this information while he is on holiday.

We use *present perfect progressive* if we want to emphasize the length of time an action has gone on continuously instead of putting particular emphasis on the result.

The *present perfect progressive* is used most often with *action verbs* such as **play, sleep, wait, work**; in other words, the same kind of verbs that are commonly found in *present progressive.*

> Why are you so late? **I've been waiting** here for hours!
> How long **have you been sitting** there, doing nothing?

Note that you can use the *present perfect progressive* to show your impatience or displeasure.

3.5 Past perfect simple and past perfect progressive

3.5.1 Past perfect simple

> I didn't watch 'Gold Rush' last night, because
> I **had** **seen** the film before.

had	Past participle

In a restaurant
'How did you find your steak, sir?' asked the waiter when the guest **had finished** eating.
'I looked under a potato chip, and there it was.'

We use the *past perfect simple* when we want to emphasize that one action or activity happened before another event in the past. If we want to say that one event in the past caused another to happen later, we often state this cause with **because** + *past perfect.*

> Caesar attacked at daybreak; his army **had marched** all night to take the enemy by surprise.
>
> The British became masters of the seas, after Nelson **(had) won** the Battle of Trafalgar.

A sequence of two or more events in the past is often linked with the conjunction **after.** *Past perfect* tense can be used in the clause following **after,** but *past simple* is acceptable too if the sequence of events is clear.
(For *past perfect* in indirect speech, see 2.3.8.)

3.5.2 Past perfect progressive

> Why didn't you come to our party last night?
> – Sorry, I was too tired.
> I **had been** **working** all day long.

Past perf. of **have**	**ing** form of verb

We use the *past perfect progressive* like the *past perfect simple*, to emphasize that one action or activity happened before another event in the past; but *past perfect progressive* indicates that it was an action or activity which continued for a period of time.

3.6 The future

English offers us several possible ways of talking about things that happen in the future. We choose between them according to the context and our intention. The different possibilities and their uses will now be described.

3.6.1 *Will*-future

	will (not)	V base	
The train	**will**	**arrive**	at 4.30 tomorrow.
OK, I	**'ll** (= will)	**meet**	you at the station.
I	**won't** (= will not)	**be**	late.

We also find **shall** instead of **will** after **I**, **we**. The shortened form of **will** is written **'ll** and pronounced /l/, while the shortened form of **will not** is written **won't** and pronounced /wəʊnt/.

Will you come alone? When **will** the game be finished?

Questions are made by simple inversion.

Tomorrow's weather **will be** cold and cloudy. There **will be** occasional showers. – Oh, no; not that again!

Will + *base* of the verb is a way of talking about the future in a neutral or objective way. It is used in *forecasts* of future events, e.g. weather forecasts, horoscopes, prophecies.

I hope the weather **will change** next week. I don't think it **will**. I'm afraid it**'ll go on** like this for a long time.

The **will**-future is common after the *present simple* tense of verbs like **think, hope, be sure, be afraid,** as a way of expressing one's opinion about the future.

Grandma: 'I've left my glasses upstairs.'
Grandson: 'Never mind. **I'll get** them for you.'

On the telephone
'Doctor, my child has just swallowed my ballpoint pen!'
'**I'll come** at once.'
'What can I do until you arrive, doctor?'
'Use a pencil.'

On Sunday I**'ll be sleeping** all day long.
While you**'re enjoying** yourself in Spain next week, I**'ll be taking** my exams.

We also use the **will**-future when we suddenly make up our mind to do something, or give a promise. We use **will** like this mainly in first person singular and plural (**I will – I'll**, **we will – we'll**). (For **if**-clauses, see 2.3.6.)

Note that there is a progressive form of the **will**-future, too (**will be** + ***ing** form of the verb). It emphasizes that an action will happen over a period of time in the future, while another action is going on. We do not use this tense, however, as much as other progressive tenses, e.g. *present progressive*.

3.6.2 *Going to*-future

We**'re going to spend** our holidays in France this summer.
– Oh, how long **are** you **going to stay**?

I**'m** not **going to learn** Russian. I think it's too difficult.

We use ***be going to*** + *base* of the verb to talk about an intention, a plan which we have already decided upon.

Stop! The rope**'s going to break**!

We also use it to talk about future consequences; that is, when we see something will cause something else to happen in the future – and usually very soon.

61

3.6.3 *Will* or *going to*?

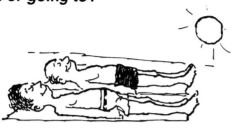

In many situations, we can use either **will** or **going to** with exactly the same meaning. But if we want to say something is very near to happening, we often prefer to use **going to.**

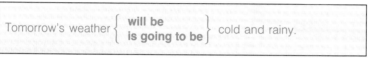

Tomorrow's weather { **will be** / **is going to be** } cold and rainy.

Look, we had better go.
It**'s going to rain**.

We often use **going to** in warnings about impending danger (see 3.17.5 and 5.11).

'Hang on! You're going to spoil the lettuces!'

Will you play cards with me?
Sorry. **I'm about to** wash my hair.

Note that **be about to** is like **be going to,** but can only be used to talk about events which will happen very soon indeed.

'My boyfriend tells everyone that he **is going to marry** the most beautiful girl in the world,' said Helen.
'I am sorry,' said Kate. 'Perhaps he **will change** his mind and **marry** you after all.'

In the joke opposite, Helen means to make a simple statement about a future which has already been decided. But Kate deliberately misunderstands the boyfriend's remark to be a strong statement of intention, i.e. a statement about something which has still to be decided. In doing so she punishes Helen for her vanity in thinking she is very beautiful. Of course, the boyfriend may change his mind; but if he does so, it will be contrary to his intention, so the ***will***-*future* is appropriate.

3.6.4 Future expressed through present progressive

Listen, dear. Mother**'s coming** to dinner **tomorrow night**.

As well as using *present progressive* tense to talk about things happening as we speak (see 3.2.5), we may use it for future events, if they are going to happen soon.

We**'re going** to Italy **next week**.
When exactly **are** you **leaving**?

When the *present progressive* is used in this way, we usually add some time expression which points to the future, e.g. **tomorrow**, **next week**, **soon**, **on Friday**.

3.6.5 Future expressed through present simple

When **does** the train **leave**?
The plane **arrives** on Monday at 10.15.
Our term **starts** at the beginning of September.

The *present simple* is only used to talk about future events when we want to refer to facts over which we have no personal control, i.e. things which are determined by calendars, timetables, programmes, etc.

3.6.6 Future perfect

We are already a long way out to sea.
Soon we **will have lost** radio contact with the shore.

will have	Past participle

We use the *future perfect* when we look forward to a moment in the future when we shall be able to look back on a completed action or activity.

63

Will you **have finished** your essay **by** next Sunday?
– No, I **won't have finished** it **until** Tuesday.
– No, but I **will have finished** it **by** Tuesday.

Sentences with verbs in *future perfect tense* often contain the prepositions **until** and **by**.

The American president **is to visit** Europe next spring.

NOTES

a) In rather formal English we also find the form **be** + **to** + *base* of the verb. You might come across this in an official announcement of some future event.

By 1983 he **would have retired** from work.
Jack said that in two years he **would have earned** enough money . . .

b) Using **would,** *future perfect* can also be set in the past, and is used in *indirect speech* too.

3.7 Auxiliary verbs

An auxiliary verb is a verb that helps another one, and as the name suggests, cannot be used on its own*. An auxiliary always accompanies a main verb.

3.7.1 Primary auxiliaries and modal auxiliaries

Has John already arrived? – No, but he**'s** just coming.
What about Jane? – I **don't** think she'll come at all.

We can divide auxiliary verbs into two categories, according to the way they function:

The *primary auxiliaries*, which are **be, do, have.** They do not change the meaning of the main verb in any way, but simply help to give the main verb its tense and aspect.

I **can** speak a little French.
You **can** have my pen.
He **may** be right.
He **must** leave immediately.

The *modal auxiliaries* are **can, could, may, might, must, ought, shall, should, will, would.** These do change or complete the meaning of the main verb which they are helping. Unlike *primary auxiliaries*, they do not have the complete range of tense forms.

* Except, of course, elliptically, e.g. *Can you see him? – Yes, I can (see him).*

3.7.2 Verbs we can use as auxiliaries and as main verbs

> I **am** a student. I **have** a room of my own.
> Have you **done** your homework?
> Do you **need** a dictionary?
> I **am** having a holiday next week.
> I'm going to tell my boss what I think of him!
> – Really? Do you **dare**?

The primary auxiliaries **be**, **do**, **have**, and in addition **need** and **dare** (see 3.13.3) may also serve as main verbs. The words which are added to them to make predicates are of several different kinds. Used as main verbs, primary auxiliaries have the full range of tense forms.

3.8 *Be* as auxiliary and as main verb

3.8.1 Forms of *be*

Present				Short forms			Past			Short forms
I	**am**	(not)	from here.	I	**'m**	(not)	I	**was**	(not) /	**was**n't.
You	**are**	(not)	English.	You	**'re**	(not) /**are**n't.	You	**were**	(not) /	**were**n't.
He				He			He			
She	**is**	(not)	too late.	She	**'s**	(not) /**is**n't.	She	**was**	(not) /	**was**n't.
It				It			It			
We				We			We			
You	**are**	(not)	going home.	You	**'re**	(not) /**are**n't.	You	**were**	(not) /	**were**n't.
They				They			They			

The non-finite forms are: base form **be**, present participle **being**, past participle **been**.

NOTES
a) Questions with **be** are always made by inversion (*S – Aux* becomes *Aux – S*) and never with **do** (see 1.2.2).
b) Imperatives: Do be quiet! Don't be afraid. (See 1.3 and 1.3.1).

> **Are** you from here?
> **Was**n't he at home?

3.8.2 Use of *be*

> **Are** you sleeping?
> He **was** called by the teacher.

As an *auxiliary*, **be** is used to form the progressive tenses and the passive.

> I'm not from here. My friend **is** English.
> She **is** happy.

As a *main verb*, **be** is used with various kinds of other words to make predicates.

3.8.3 *There* + *be*

> **There is** someone there.
> **There are** some magazines on the table.
> **There were** no pictures on the walls.
> **There was** one record which we often listened to.

In this sentence pattern, the real subject is held back and introduced by **There + be** (**is**, **are**; **was**, **were**) i.e. There is **someone** at the door = **Someone** is at the door. (*S* = someone).

Notice that we find **there + be** typically in sentences which contain *adverbials of place*, especially prepositional phrases.

Some languages also permit free use of sentences like: On the table are magazines. Although this pattern exists in English, too, its place is mainly in novels, etc. and it is better avoided in everyday English.

> **There is** no reason to be angry.
> **There were** no tickets left.
> **There was** no water.

We also find **there + be** in sentences which do not contain *adverbials of place*. In sentences like: There was no water. there may be no words after the real subject at all; we can understand this sentence as meaning: No water existed there.

3.9 *Have* as auxiliary and as main verb

3.9.1 Forms of *have*

Present affirmative	Present negative
I, You { **have** / **'ve*** } seen him.	I, You { **have not** / **'ve not*** / **haven't*** } seen him
He, She, It { **has** / **'s*** } gone.	He, She, It { **has not** / **hasn't*** / **'s not*** } gone.
We, You, They { **have** / **'ve*** } got some money.	He, You, They { **have not** / **haven't*** } got any money.

In the *past tense* we use **had ('d)** in all persons. For negatives: **had ('d) not /hadn't**.

The non-finite forms of **have** are: base form **have**; present participle **having**; and past participle **had**.

* Short forms

66

He'd been waiting.
I had not heard of him.

3.9.2 Use of *have*

Have you ever **read** Robinson Crusoe?
He said he**'d** never **read** it before.

Our friends **have** a holiday flat near Brighton.
Have they a motorboat, too? – Yes, they **have**.
Their boat **has** lights which they use in fog.
Does the boat **have** sails? – No, it **doesn't**.

As an *auxiliary*, we use **have** to form the *present perfect* and *past perfect* tenses (see 3.4. and 3.5).

We can also use **have** as a *main verb* with the meaning **own** or **possess**. To make a question with **have** as main verb, we can either simply invert subject and verb, i.e. **They have ...** becomes **Have they ...?**, or we can use the auxiliary **Do: Do they have ...?**
   We cannot use the verb **have** in progressive tenses if it has the meaning of possession or ownership, because these are states, not actions.

Four negatives to choose from:

He **has** no car. = He **doesn't have** a car. =
He **hasn't got** a car. = He **hasn't** a car.

Have you **got** a moped? – No, I **haven't**.
I **have**n't **got** enough money to buy one.
Have you **got** a ruler? I've left mine at home.

In BrE, in questions and negatives especially, **have got** is used more often than **have** on its own. This is particularly true of questions and negatives which refer to the situation at the actual moment of speaking, e.g. Have you got enough money (with you at the moment)?
   The meanings of **have got** and **have** (possession) are identical.

In AmE especially, **have** is more common than **have got**. Question and negative in AmE are usually formed with **do** (see 1.2.1 and 1.2.4).

Do they **have a caravan**?

> I **had**n't **(got)** enough money to buy a new camera.
> **Did** you **have** a pet when you were a child?
> —Yes, I **had** a hamster.

> I hope I**'ll have** enough money for a car when I'm 18.

3.9.3 *Have* as action verb*

> Is Tom in?
> Yes, he is. He's just **having lunch**.
> Would you like to **have a cup of tea** with us?
> When do you **have supper**?
> You'll feel better when you**'ve had** a bath.

'*I'm worn out. Couldn't we have a rest here?*'

3.10 *Do* as auxiliary and as main verb

3.10.1 Forms of *do*

	Present	Short forms
I You He	**do** (not) /	**do**n't
She It	**does** (not) /	**does**n't
We You They	**do** (not) /	**do**n't

In past tense, **had got** is common enough, but we use **had** by itself more often. In questions, **Did you have ...?** is used more or less exclusively.

In all other tenses except present and past, **have** is used on its own i.e. without **got**. (But for **have (got) to = must**, see 3.13.)

In a number of idiomatic expressions, *have* + *noun* describes an activity, e.g. **have breakfast**. On these occasions we are using **have** as an action verb, with its meaning of **take, receive**, etc. In this situation, progressive forms are available to us. Now **do**, not inversion, is used to form questions.

Some of the most common idioms with **have** are: **have a bath, have a drink, have a guess, have a look, have a shower, have a swim, have a good time, have a try** (also, with the same meaning, **have a go**).

Note that the present perfect form of *have* + *noun* is **have had ('ve had)**.

(For **have something done** = 'get something done', see note in 2.3.13.)

In the *past tense*, all persons take **did (not)/didn't**. The present participle is **doing**, the past participle **done**.

Pronunciation
do /duː/   **don't** /dəʊnt/
does /dəz/ (weak) or /dʌz/ (strong)   **doesn't** /dʌznt/

3.10.2 Use of *do*

Do you speak French? – No, I **do**n't.

We use **do** as an *auxiliary* with main verbs to form questions and negatives (see 1.2, 1.4).
(For short answers, see 1.4.6.)
(For emphatic use, see 1.3.)

First, I must **do** my homework, and then I can **do** the washing-up.

Do is also used as a main verb in idiomatic expressions such as **do one's homework** (i.e. write or learn it), **do someone a favour, do science at school** (i.e. learn science), **do the washing-up** (i.e. wash up).

3.11 *Can/be able to*

3.11.1 Forms of *can/be able to*

I
He } **can** play the guitar, but I **cannot** (= can't) play the violin.

In the *present tense*, all persons have the form **can**. (NB. No **s** at the end of 3rd person singular!) The normal pronunciation is /kən/, but if the word is emphasized, it becomes /kæn/. The negative form is written as one word. The shortened form of **cannot** is **can't**, which in BrE is pronounced /kɑːnt/, but in AmE /kænt/.

She **could** play the piano, although she **could not** (= couldn't) read the notes.

In the *past tense*, all persons have **could**. Normal pronunciation /kəd/, but /kʊd/ if emphasized. Negative: **could not.** Shortened form: **couldn't**.

I **can't** read Arabic writing, but Jill **can.**
I **could** see the forest, but I **couldn't** see the river.

In a compound sentence we don't need to repeat the main verb after **can** or **could**, if we can leave out the object, too. But if there is a new object, we have to repeat the main verb.

Form of **be**	**able**	**to +** infinitive

You can't drive a car now, but you'll **be able to** (**drive** one) when you're older.

He **hadn't been able to walk** for many years, because of an accident he had had in a car.

The *modal auxiliary* **can** only has two forms, the present tense, **can** and the past tense **could.** If we need to express possibility in some other tense, we have to get round the problem by using a substitute. The most usual way round the problem is to use **be able.** This, as you see, contains the verb **be,** and so is available in any tense (see 3.11.2).

3.11.2 Use of *can/be able to*

I **can** speak English quite well, but I **cannot** speak French.
She is old and **can't** walk far nowadays.

We use **can** to talk about *ability* and *capability*: our skills, our knowledge, things we know how to do (well). On the other hand, **cannot/can't** is used to express *inability* and *incapability.*

'Of course I'm OK. Hand me back my hockey stick, so I can get back in the game.'

I **could** already read at the age of 5.

In the *past tense*, we use **could** only when we are talking about a skill, e.g. reading, in a general way.

We **were able** to finish our homework by 6 o'clock.
Will you **be able** to finish your paper by Friday?
– No, I'm afraid I won't.

When we are talking about one particular achievement, on the other hand, we must use **was/were able** instead of **could.**
   In all other tenses we use the relevant form of **be able**.

Can you help me move house? – I **could** come round and do some packing tomorrow, if you like.

Could in this and many other examples includes a sense of **if I have to/had to,** whereas **be able to** always includes a sense of success, i.e. We were able to finish = We succeeded in finishing; but I could read = I knew how to read, when necessary.

Can I leave you for a moment? – Of course, you **can**.
           – Sorry, you **can't** leave now.
Could I leave early today? Would you mind?

A further use of **can/could** is to ask for *permission*. With this meaning, **could** may also be used to talk about the present or future, and is considered more polite than **can**. As you would expect from the above, **cannot/can't** are used to refuse permission (see 3.13.1).

(For **may/be allowed to**, see 3.12.)

'Couldn't you read something else for a change?'

Do you think this ring **could** be gold?
– It **can't** be gold, it's too light.

Can and **could** also both refer to the present in a third use, which is to talk about *possibility*. If **could** is used, it indicates greater doubt, or less certainty than use of **can**.

It's no good waiting for John any longer.
– Well, let's wait a few more minutes, he **could** have missed the bus.

By using **could** with the *perfect infinitive* we can make assumptions about the past.

You **could** at least have waited a bit, couldn't you?

The combination **could** + *perfect infinitive* is also a way of reproaching someone for something they did (or didn't do).

'I **can** meet you at ten,' he said. → He said he **could** meet me at ten.

Could is used in place of **can** in *indirect speech*, when the speech occurred in the past (see 2.3.8).

3.12 *May/be allowed to*

May we watch the film on TV tonight?
– Yes, you **may.**
– No, you **may** not, we've got guests.
He **may** not leave yet.

We use **may** to ask for *permission* and to grant it; and we use **may not** to refuse permission.
    Of course, **can** may also be used for this purpose, e.g. Can I have your pencil (please)?; but **may** is perhaps regarded as more polite. (In former times, it was also regarded as more correct, but this is no longer true.)

'You **may** go now.'　　He said I **might** go.

In present tense only, **may** is sometimes a polite way in which a superior gives an inferior permission to leave if he expects him to do so, i.e. the superior in effect dismisses the inferior with You may go now. In this use, **might** is available only in *indirect speech*.

	Form of **be** (not)	**allowed**	**to** + infinitive
You	**are** not	**allowed**	**to** smoke here.
We	**were**n't	**allowed**	**to** go out.
He said the			
children	**had** not **been**	**allowed**	**to** stay out late.
I	**'ll** (= will) **be**	**allowed**	**to** drive a motorbike next year.

If we need to talk about permission in any other tense except the present, we must use a substitute for **may/might,** and the commonest alternative is **be allowed to.**

　　Be allowed can be understood as the passive form of the verb **allow,** i.e. My parents didn't **allow** me to stay out late = I **wasn't allowed** to stay out late (by my parents).

(For speakers' intentions see 3.17.2.)

We'd better fill the tank up. We **may not** get to another petrol station for the next few hours. – OK, you **may** be right.

Finally, **may** is used to say what we *assume, expect* or *guess* about present or future happenings.

Where's John?
– He **may have missed** the bus again.

With *may + perfect infinitive* we can offer a possible explanation of something that has not happened as expected.

It's late, but he **might** still turn up.
He **might have missed** the train, you know.

With **might** we can express a hope or make a speculation which seems rather unlikely to be true.

'You **may** borrow my car,' she said. → She said I **might** borrow her car.

Might is used in place of **may** in indirect speech, when the speech occurred in the past (see 2.3.8).

3.13 *Must/have to/need (not)*

3.13.1 *Must*

'And he must stay in the cellar until he says sorry . . .'

We use **must** to talk about *necessity* or *obligation*. This verb only has a present tense, and all persons have the same form (**must**).

If we wish to talk about necessity or obligation in any other tense we must use the substitute **have to.** This is available in present tense too, and so is its variant, **have got to.**

(There is one exception to the above rule: **must** may be used in a past context in reported speech, e.g. She said she must pay for it.)

Must I help in the kitchen today?

– No, { you **needn't**.
{ you **don't need to**.

– No, { you **don't have to**.
{ you **haven't got to**.

There are two negative forms of **must,** and they are used differently. We use **mustn't** when there is a duty to not do something; when in fact, it would be wrong to do it. We use **needn't** when there is no duty. We can also use **don't need to/don't have to/haven't got to** instead of **needn't**.

I'm going to open my present now!
– No, you **mustn't**. We're all going to open them together, this evening.

You **mustn't** park here. Can't you see the sign?

Using **mustn't** /mʌsnt/ is a strong way of *forbidding* a course of action, or *advising against* it. This may either be something which is generally forbidden or inadvisable, or something which is forbidden or inadvisable on a particular occasion, or in a particular set of circumstances.

> We **mustn't** forget our passports.
> I'm never going to speak to John again.
> – Oh, no. You **mustn't** say that. He'll apologize, and you'll be friends again, you'll see.

Because **mustn't** is a strong expression, you shouldn't use it too often.

To *refuse permission* you can say: No, you **can't/may not.**

You can soften a refusal by adding words such as: I'm (very) sorry./I'm afraid./No, I'm sorry, you can't./No, you may not, I'm afraid.

If you want to *warn* someone or *advise* them strongly against doing something, you can say: **Please don't** ... or **You shouldn't** ... This sounds warmer than **mustn't,** and is just as effective.

'There must be some reason he's so angry.'

> We haven't seen Tom at college for more than a week now. He **must be** ill or on holiday.
> (There can't be any other explanation, surely?)

A further special use of **must** is to express *conclusions* and *assumptions* from known facts.

> His telephone bill is huge!
> He **must spend** a lot of time on the phone.
> (There's no other way of explaining such a large bill.)

In this use, **must** usually combines with **be,** but sometimes with other verbs.

> Where's Jack? – I don't know. He **must have missed** the train.
> – But he **cannot/can't** have missed the train.

Similarly to the above, **must** combines with **have been** and other perfect infinitives to draw conclusions about past events. To reject such conclusions we use **cannot/can't.**

3.13.2 *Have to*

*'What do I think? – I'm king ...
I don't have to think.'*

When we use **have to** as a substitute for **must** it is often treated as a main verb. (In fact, in AmE it is almost always treated so.) This means that negatives and questions are formed with **do/did** as an auxiliary.

There is an alternative, and that is to treat **have to** as an auxiliary, and so make questions by inversion, and negatives by adding **n't** to the appropriate part of **have.** But this is done less frequently.

	positive	question	negative
Present	We **have to** go.	Do we **have to** go? (**Have** we **to** go?)	We don't **have to** go. (We **haven't to** go.)
Past	We **had to** go.	Did we **have to** go?	We didn't **have to** go.
Future	We'**ll have to** go.	Will we **have to** go?	We **won't** (= will not) **have to** go.

In all tenses except present, **must** is not available, and we must use **have to** instead (see 3.13.1).

However, **have to** is also available as an alternative to **must** in the present tense. So is **have got to.** Both these verbs suggest that it is outside circumstances which make a certain action necessary.

Sorry, I couldn't come. We **had to** do a lot of homework yesterday.
I see. Well, I'll **have to** write an essay this weekend.
Did we **have to** answer these questions?
– No, we **didn't.** We just **had to** read them through.
We **have got to** answer them in class, next lesson.

In everyday speech, **have got to** can sound rather stronger than **have to.** It is used in preference to **must** when something beyond our control, e.g. a timetable, regulations, etc., forces us to take a particular course of action.

'Noah! You've got to keep the elephants still!'

Sorry, I can't play with you now. – I'**ve got to** do my homework first.
– I **must** do my homework first.

In the first example, homework is seen as a circumstance beyond the speaker's control. In the second example, he feels himself obliged to do it.

3.13.3 *Need (not)*

Needn't as an *auxiliary* occurs only in the present tense. It is followed by an infinitive without **to.** The meaning is **don't have to** or **it isn't necessary to.**

Needn't as an *auxiliary* occurs often in negative answers to questions which begin **Must I/We ...?** (see 3.13.1).

You **needn't** copy the words.
Just try to remember them.

> **Do** we **need to** ⎫
> **Need** we ⎬ bring our schoolbags tomorrow?
>
> No, you ⎰ **don't need to.**
> ⎱ **needn't.**

> You ⎰ **needn't** ⎱ be rich to be burgled.
> ⎱ **don't need to** ⎰
> I **didn't need to** look up any words.

> Do we **need** our passports?
> I think you'll **need** an umbrella.
> I don't **need** your help, thank you.

In addition, **need** may be used as a *main verb*, and then questions and negatives are made with **do**, and the infinitive is preceded by **to**. The meaning of **Do we need?** is the same as **Need we?**, and **don't need to** means the same as **needn't**.

In the present tense there is a choice of negative forms, **needn't** or **don't need to**. In the past tense there is, in modern colloquial English, only one form, **didn't need to**. (The form **needed not to** is no longer in use.)

Note that the main verb **need** also has the meaning **require** and is then followed by a noun object.

3.14 *Shall/should/ought to*

3.14.1 *Shall/should*

'What shall I do now, dear? I can't sit up here all night while you read the paper.'

> **Shall** I make tea or coffee?
> **Shall** we go?

In everyday language we use **shall** almost exclusively in the first person **(I, we),** and its main function is to ask other people what they wish us to do (or not to do). Normal pronunciation of **shall** is /ʃəl/, but when it is emphasized, /ʃæl/; **shan't** /ʃɑːnt/.

> Don't worry. He **shall** not trouble you again. (= You **shan't** be troubled again.)
> It **shan't** happen again.
> I shall leave tomorrow, and you **shan't** ever see me again!

Just occasionally we may find **shall** with future reference, in second or third person. The function then is to make promises or threats. (For **shall** as future, see 3.6.1.)

We use **should** /ʃəd/ (when emphasized /ʃʊd/ and its negative **shouldn't** in order to find out the wishes of others; and also when we want their advice, or when we'd like to give them our advice, or make suggestions. Unlike **shall**, which is limited to the first person, **should** can have a subject which is first, second or third person.

Should I bring my records to your party?
Should the children bring their raincoats?

When it has this meaning, **should** cannot be used in *past tense*. Instead, we have to make use of expressions such as **be supposed to, be expected to,** and **be to**.

Form of be (not)	supposed expected	to infinitive
They didn't give us a key.		
– So how **were** we { supposed expected }		**to** get into the building?
How **was** I		**to** know the door was unlocked?

Nobody wants to help me, so what **am** I **to do?**
Are we **to** wait for an answer?

Note that the expression **be to** is available when we are entirely dependent on other people's decisions.

He
You } **should** work a little harder.
And you really **shouldn't** smoke so much.

Observations of this kind are in the nature of *warnings, complaints* or *good advice*.

By using **should** + *perfect infinitive* we can say that we now think a decision we took was a wrong one. We can also criticize the decisions of others.

'We **shouldn't have left** the marked path.'

> It's 11.30. Mary **should** be in London by now.
> There **shouldn't** be any problems. The test won't be difficult.

We can use **should** to express reasonable assumptions.
(For **should** in *if*-clauses, see 2.3.7.)
(For **should** in *indirect speech*, see 2.3.9.)

3.14.2 *Ought to*

> We **oughtn't to** have left the marked track.
> You **ought to** be more careful next time.
> They **ought to** have arrived by now.
> He **oughtn't to** be short of money. I lent him £100.

We can use **ought to** as an alternative to **should** to give advice, to criticize ourselves and others, and to say that we think something is probable (or improbable).
   Ought to is rather more emphatic than **should.**
   After **ought** we must always have **to** + *infinitive.* The *present infinitive* is used in statements about present and future; the *perfect infinitive* for statements about the past.

3.15 *Will/would*

3.15.1 Forms of *will/would*

Will is used in all persons.
Shortened to: **'ll,** e.g. **I'll** marry you, if **you'll** let me.

Won't /wəʊnt/ is the shortened form of negative **will not.** It is common in spoken English and also in some kinds of writing, e.g. personal letters.

> **Will** you marry me?
> – No, I **won't.** I want to be free.

Would /wʊd/ is used in all persons, too. Shortened to: **'d,** e.g. **I'd** prefer to be free.

wouldn't is the shortened form of the negative **would not.**

I asked him if he **would** marry me. But he said he **wouldn't.**

3.15.2 Use of *will/would*

Will you marry me?

As a *modal auxiliary*, **will** expresses a definite intention, a firm decision. (Will you marry me? is a serious proposal!)

Other verbs which have this meaning are **want, intend, be willing to.**

Whether **will** has this meaning of a definite intention depends very much on the context. In fact, this meaning is often hard to distinguish from a plain statement about what will happen in the future, and it is of course identical in form to the *future simple* tense (see 3.6.1).

I'll be back on time.
We **won't** stay long.

NOTES
When listening to English, be careful not to mistake **won't**/wəʊnt/ for **want** /wɒnt/, and vice versa.

I **want** to go to England next year.
I **won't** go to England next year.

Will you please follow me?
Will you leave your coats in the hall?

We also use **will** in polite requests and invitations.

Won't you come in and sit down, Mr Harker?

In a request or invitation, the negative form **won't** sounds even more friendly than **will.** The expectation of a positive answer is greater (see 1.4.4).

Jonathan **will** be in Transylvania by now. He **will** probably **have arrived** at Dracula's castle, **if** all has gone well.

We can use **will** in making an assumption or a prediction, if we are fairly certain about it.
(See also **must be,** 3.13.1.) Such predictions are often accompanied by **if** -clauses (see 2.3.7).

I keep asking Tommy to shut the door, but he **will** leave it open.
We tried to warn him, but he **wouldn't** listen.
I tried to stop him, but he **would** go.
He said he **would** continue his journey, whatever happened.

We use **will** and **would** (also **won't** and **wouldn't**) to say that someone was unwilling to take our advice.
In *indirect speech,* **would** is the *past tense* equivalent of **will** when it is used to express an intention (see 2.3.9).

Would you like to have tea with me?
Would you read this letter, please?

We also use **would** in *polite requests, invitations* and *wishes.*

I'd like to return to England as soon as possible.

Note that we find **would** in a number of phrases used to express preferences, such as **I'd like to, I would prefer to, I'd rather** (see 1.1.3.2).

3.16 *Used to*

There **used to** be a nice old pub on that corner.
I **used to** play darts there once a week but I **didn't use to** win very often.

Used to /ˈjuːstə/ is a way of talking about habits or other regular activities in the past. (A more formal equivalent of **We used to** . . . is It was our regular practice to . . .)

The usual negative form of **used to** is **didn't use to**.

But remember that *past simple* is also used to talk about habits or regular activities in the past, especially when combined with **always** and expressions like **every day, on Sundays,** e.g. We always went to church on Sundays when I was a child.

We **used to** go hiking every weekend. We **would** walk for hours and hours and then ...

You'll soon **get used to** driving on the left-hand side.

Note that in narratives, **would** is sometimes used to continue a story which began with **used to.** The meaning is the same.

Don't confuse the **used to** we are discussing here with the expression **be/become/get used to,** which means 'find easier with practice', or 'find less strange with experience'.

3.17 Modals used to serve various communicative purposes

In sections 3.11 to 3.16 we looked at each of the *modal auxiliaries* from the points of view of its forms and its various uses. However, when we are actually talking, form isn't usually the uppermost thing in our minds. We are more concerned with the need to communicate a particular idea; for example, an intention, or a suggestion.

If we want to communicate efficiently, we need to be aware of the various possible ways which we can choose from in order to express the idea we have in mind. And further, we need to know which of the various ways is most appropriate to our particular situation at the time.

In sections 3.17.1 to 3.17.6 we are therefore going to give you a survey of ways in which some important communicative purposes can be achieved (in simpler terms, how you can be sure you are saying things the way you want to say them). In each section you will find not only the *modal auxiliary* or *auxiliaries* which express a particular purpose, but also a number of other idiomatic expressions which have the same function.

Please note that there is further information about how to achieve various communicative purposes in section 5.

3.17.1 Certainty – uncertainty

That **must** be the right way.
They **must** have taken a short-cut.
There **has to** be another way.
(There's **got to** be ...)
This **can't** be the right way.
Let's ask the bus driver. He **will** (= must) know.

In the examples opposite, various *modals* express different degrees of certainty or uncertainty about the facts which are stated.

These *modals* can be arranged on a scale, with **must** (= greatest certainty) at one end and **might** (= greatest uncertainty) at the other:

Other expressions:

I am { **sure** } this is(n't) the right way.
{ **certain** } they have taken a short-cut.

Surely this isn't the right way?

must	High degree of
have (got) to	certainty
can't	
couldn't	

There **will certainly** be another way.	will would	

We { **should** / **ought to** } get there in time. And about events in the past: They { **should** / **ought to** } **have arrived** there by now.	should ought to	Not so certain, but probable

Other expressions:
We'**ll probably**
We **are likely to** } get there in time.
It'**s likely** that we will

This **could** be the road to the station. **Can** this really be the right way?	can could	Stating or questioning a doubtful possibility

Other expressions:
It'**s possible** that this is the right way to the station.
Possibly this is the right way.

They **may** come on the next train. They **may** have missed the train.	may	Even less certain, but possible

Other expressions:
It'**s possible** that they will come on the next train.
Perhaps they will come on the next train.

They **might** come on the next train. They **might** have missed the road.	might	Still just possible, but very uncertain; uncertainty

Other expressions:
It'**s possible** . . . (but I don't think it likely).

3.17.2 Permission – prohibition

| Can
May
Could | I have a look at your map? – Yes, of course you { can.
may. |

Can, **could** and **may** are used in questions which are requests for permission.

Could and **may** are considered to be a little more formal and polite than **can**.

Permission is given with **can** or **may**.

You { can
may } use my guidebook.

Other expressions:

Would you mind { if I opened
my opening } the window?

Do you mind { if I read
my reading } your letter?

Are we allowed to use our dictionaries?
Would it be all right if I came late?
Is it all right/OK if I do it tomorrow?

'Could you go to Earth with him?
I'm going shopping.'

You $\begin{Bmatrix} \textbf{can't} \\ \textbf{may not} \end{Bmatrix}$ smoke in here.

You **mustn't** park here, (I'm afraid).

Permission is refused, and prohibitions are made, with **can't**, **may not**, **mustn't**. These are softened by using **I'm sorry** or **I'm afraid**.

Instead of giving a point-blank refusal, it is often a good idea to make a suggestion, e.g. not You mustn't park here, but Why don't you park somewhere else? (see 3.17.5).

Other expressions:

You **aren't allowed to** park here.

It is $\begin{Bmatrix} \textbf{not permitted} \\ \textbf{forbidden} \end{Bmatrix}$ to park here.

You **are not to talk** during the test.

3.17.3 Requests ·

Can
Could $\Big\}$ you help me, please?

Would you please pass me the salt?

Will you post this letter for me, please?

We can use **can**, **could**, **would** and **will** to make *requests*.

Other expressions:

Would you be kind and shut the window?

Would you mind shutting the window?

3.17.4 Offers, suggestions and invitations

Won't you come in and sit down?
Would(n't) you like to have a cup of tea?
Shall I get you some biscuits?
Will you have dinner with us?
Can I do anything to help you?
Could you come to supper on Thursday?

Auxiliaries which we can use to make *offers*, *suggestions* and *invitations* are **shall**, **will**, **won't** and **wouldn't**, and also **can/could**.

Where **can** we get a decent meal in this town?
Where **could** one spend an hour or two while waiting for a bus?

We can also use **can** or **could** to ask for a suggestion.

Other expressions:
What ⎫
How ⎬ **about** having a drink?
Let's have a drink.
Let me carry your bag for you.
Why don't we take a taxi?
I'll do it for you, shall I?

3.17.5 Advice and warnings

What ⎰ **shall** ⎱ I do?
⎱ **should** ⎰
How **can** I mend this vase?
What **would** you do if you were in my position?

You ⎰ **should** ⎱ talk to your teacher.
⎱ **ought to** ⎰

We can use **shall**, **should**, **can**, **could** and **would** *to ask for advice*.
To give advice we can use **should** and **ought to**. But remember that **ought to** is a very strong form of recommendation.

Other expressions:
You **had better** go and see your teacher about it.
If I were you I'd ask my teacher about it.
I'd advise you to go and talk to him.
You**'d better not** sit so close to the fire.

The expressions on the left and in the box above may also serve as *warnings*, or even *threats*, if a high falling intonation tune is used. The speaker's face will probably look very serious and he may wag his finger.

If **you don't stop** making that noise, I'll call the police.
Stop that noise **or** I'll call the police!
You**'d better** hold on tight, you're going to fall!

We often follow *warnings* by saying something unpleasant will happen if they are not heeded.

3.17.6 Commands

You **must** go to bed now.
You'**ll have to** get up early tomorrow.
You **mustn't** forget your ticket.
(= Don't forget your ticket.)

The modals we most often use to express *commands* are **have (got) to** and (for prohibitions) **mustn't**.

However, for the sake of politeness or good relations (e.g. with employees or students), we often prefer to give commands in the form of *advice, suggestions* and *requests* (see 3.17.3, 3.17.4 and 3.17.5).

Other expressions:
He says we **are to** wait for the manager.
Do you **want us to** read this through?
We **were told to** wait here.

4 The noun phrase

4.1 Nouns

4.1.1 Forms of the noun

Singular	Plural				
	Pronunciation /s/	/z/	/ɪz/	*Spelling*
one hat two hats a month six months				s
a dog young dogs one shoe a pair of shoes				
a sandwich sandwiches a box some boxes one page ten pages				es

We normally form the plurals of nouns by adding **s** to the singular form.

But after sibilants (s, z, ʃ, ʒ, tʃ, dʒ) we add **es**, unless the singular form already ends in a silent **e**. The pronunciation of **es** is /ɪz/.

Pronunciation: /s/ after voiceless consonants /p, t, k, f, θ/
                   /z/ after voiced consonants /b, d, g, m, v, ð/ and vowels
                   /ɪz/ after sibilants /s, z, ʃ, ʒ, tʃ, dʒ/

Peculiarities of spelling and pronunciation:

this country → most countries

y after a consonant becomes **ie**. But note: **boy** → **boys**.

my kni**fe**	– our kni**ves**	/naɪf, naɪvz/
a housewi**fe**	– housewi**ves**	/-waɪf, -waɪvz/
my bookshel**f**	– new bookshel**ves**	/-ʃelf, -ʃelvz/
a thie**f**	– some thie**ves**	/θiːf, θiːvz/
a lea**f**	– autumn lea**ves**	/liːf, liːvz/
a scar**f**	– red scar**ves**	/skɑːf, skɑːvz/
a brown loa**f**	– brown loa**ves**	/ləʊf, ləʊvz/

Some words end in **f** or **fe** (pronounced /f/) in the singular, but take the plural ending **ves** (pronounced /vz/).

*Some grammars use the term *substantive* instead of *noun*.

a hot ba**th**	– too many hot ba**ths**	/bɑːθ, bɑːðz/
mou**th**	– open your mou**ths**	/maʊθ, maʊðz/
pa**th**	– different pa**ths**	/pɑːθ, pɑːðz/

Some nouns which end with the letters **th** and which have a long vowel or diphthong, are pronounced differently in singular and plural: singular /θ/, plural /ðz/.

a potat**o**	– a pound of potat**oes** ·	/pəˈteɪtəʊz/
a her**o**	– the her**oes** of the Western	/ˈhɪərəʊz/
a radi**o**	– many radi**os**	/ˈreɪdɪəʊz/

Some nouns ending in **o** have the plural ending **es**, but this does not apply to words which have come into the English language in the last 150 years or so, such as pian**o**, radi**o**, phot**o**. The pronunciation of **os** and **oes** in these plurals is the same, /z/.

a hou**se**	– modern hou**ses**	/haʊs, haʊzɪz/

The noun **house** also changes pronunciation in the plural.

one **man**	– three **men**	/mæn, /men/
a police**man**	– some police**men**	/pəˈliːsmən, pəˈliːsmən/
woman	– **women**	/wʊmən, wɪmɪn/
mouse	– **mice**	/maʊs, maɪs/
goose	– **geese**	/guːs, giːs/
my **foot**	– my **feet**	/fʊt, fiːt/
a bad **tooth**	– bad **teeth**	/tuːθ, tiːθ/
a new **penny**	– no· **pennies**	/ˈpeni, ˈpenɪz/
	– it costs six **pence** (6p)	/pens/

Some nouns have *irregular plural forms*, involving a change of vowel.

In the old British currency, the 240th part of a pound (one twelfth of a shilling) was called a **penny** and this had the irregular plural **pence**. However, since decimalization (i.e. since £1 (one pound) = 100p), most people in Britain refer to the coins as **one p** /wʌn piː/, **two p** /tuː piː/.

Why do white sheep eat more than black ones?

Because there are more of them.

a **child**	– a lot of **children**
ox	– **oxen**
a **sheep**	– a flock of **sheep**
a **fish**	– a lot of **fish**

The plurals of **child** and **ox** also have irregular plurals. A few nouns are the same in singular and plural. (You may sometimes come across **fishes** as a plural of **fish**, too).

road sign	– road **signs**
passer-by	– **passers**-by
grown-up	– grown-**ups**

With *compound nouns* composed of two nouns, like **road sign(s)**, it is the second noun (the base noun) which receives the plural ending. If the compound contains only one noun, the position of the plural ending may vary.

4.1.2 Case forms of the noun

> He gave **the monkey a banana**.
> He gave **a banana to the monkey**.

> Our parent**s'** idea of fun was a long walk in the country.
> Young people**'s** interests have changed a lot these days.

> The boy**'s**
> The boy**s'**
> The children**'s** } ball.
> James**'s**
> My dog**'s** name is Ronnie.

Some languages have different endings to the noun to show whether it is acting as a subject, a direct object, or an indirect object, etc.

English nouns are available in only one form for subject and object (the *common case*), plus a *possessive* (see below).

In English the function of a noun (as subject, object, etc.) is shown by word order, i.e. its position in the sentence (see 1.1.4), or by use of a preposition (see 4.5.18).

The *possessive* is formed by adding **s** to the noun to show possession.

Forms
Singular: **'s**
Plural ending in **s** or **es**: **-'**
Irregular plural: **'s**
Names ending in **s**: **'s**

Whose book is this? – It is my **friend's**.
  – (It's) **John's**.

First we bought this bread **at the baker's**, and then we went **to the chemist's**.

Let's visit **St Paul's** (Cathedral).
Can we go on foot?
– Well, we could, but it is an **hour's** walk.

Let's have our picnic on top **of** the hill.
Have you got a road map **of** Ireland?

Use

The *possessive* in **'s** is in general use with people and animals (especially domestic pets and other smaller animals). It indicates possession or that things belong together, e.g. **boys' work** (= work for boys).

The pronunciation of the *possessive* ending **'s** (the **dog's** /dɒgz/ name, the **cat's** /kæts/ name) depends on the consonant which precedes it, as in the case of plurals of nouns (see 4.1.1).

Nouns with the *possessive* ending **'s** may stand on their own, without the word they actually refer to, e.g. It's **John's**. = It's **John's book**.

The noun to which the *possessive* refers is also missing in expressions like: at the **baker's**, to the **doctor's**. These are understood to mean at the **baker's** (shop), to the **doctor's** (surgery), etc.

As well as geographical references like **St Paul's** (Cathedral), in which the *possessive* **'s** is attached to a personal name, we also find **'s** after names of countries, towns and cities, and institutions: **Britain's** coloured immigrants, **London's** buses, the **Government's** proposal.

We also use the *possessive* with **'s** in many time expressions such as: an **hour's** walk, a **week's** holiday (= a holiday of a week), **today's** programme (= the programme of/for today).

Another form of *possessive* is made with the preposition **of**. This form is correct when the noun it refers to is not a person or an animal.

A group **of** tourists visited our town.
Do you know the name **of** the boy who is standing over there?

That's Alex. He's a friend **of** my brother**'s**.

Alison is coming to the disco with David.
He's a friend **of hers**.

We also use the *possessive* with **of** when we mention a quantity (**a group of**, **a number of**), or when we want to put a relative clause after the possessive noun.

In complex noun phrases a *double possessive* is sometimes necessary or convenient. (He's a friend of my brother's. = He's one of my brother's friends.)

If a pronoun comes after the *possessive* with **of** it has to be a *possessive pronoun* (e.g. **hers**) and not a *subject* or *object pronoun* (**she**, **her**, etc.). (He's a friend of hers. = He's one of her friends.)

4.1.3 Kinds of noun

A holiday at the Machrie Hotel means fun for the whole family: rooms with TV, games, afternoon tea, music.
Special rates from Sept.–March, and at Easter and Christmas.

The following definitions will help you to understand the use of nouns:

Proper nouns (names) are used to describe people, countries, places etc., months of the year, days of the week, and feast days: **the Machrie Hotel**, **the Isle of Skye**, **March**, **Christmas**, **Susan** and **Mr Smith**.

Common nouns are, broadly speaking, all the rest.

The majority of common nouns are *countable*. This means they can form both singular and plural, and can have a definite or an indefinite article in front of them: **a holiday**, **rooms**, **the family**, **games**.

Other common nouns are *uncountable*. *Uncountable nouns* are so-called because they are normally used in the singular, and without an article: **fun**, **tea**, **music**.

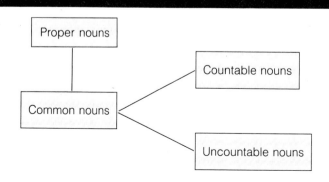

> **Swimming** is good for you.
> He has given all his **savings** to help the poor.

We make some nouns by adding **ing** to the *base of a verb* (see 1.1.2 and 1.1.3.1). Such words are normally uncountable if they mean the activity, e.g. **swimming**, but may be countable, if they mean the outcome of an activity, e.g. **savings**.

4.1.4 Uncountable nouns

> Real wooden **furniture** is expensive these days.
> That cupboard is a valuable **piece of furniture**.
> He brought his **equipment** with him: a hammer, a saw, a blow-lamp, and a small pump.
> Can you give me any **information** about **accommodation** in this city?
> The **news** today is rather dull, but there is one interesting **item**.

Uncountable nouns have no plural form, therefore the verbs following them are always singular, and any determiner must also be singular (i.e. we can use **this**, **that** with them, but never **these**, **those**, **many**).

Uncountable nouns cannot combine with the indefinite articles **a**, **an**, nor with any number words (**one**, **ten**, etc.). In addition to words like **furniture**, **equipment**, uncountable nouns include a variety of *abstract nouns* such as **advice**, **evidence**, **homework**, **information**, **knowledge**, **help**, **progress**.

A small number of words are regarded as being *uncountable* in English, when other languages regard them as *countable*. If we need to count them, we place a countable *classifier* in front of them, e.g. four **items/pieces** of equipment; an interesting **bit/item/piece** of news.

There are occasional differences between BrE and AmE usage: for example in AmE **accommodation** is treated as a *countable noun*.

Among *uncountable nouns* there are some ending in **s**. These are things which, although they have many parts, are thought of as a whole. In this group there is **news**, as well as the names of various academic subjects (**mathematics**, **physics**, **economics**, etc.) and certain games, e.g. **darts**.

> **Mathematics** isn't my strong point.
> **Darts** is very popular in Britain.

He has a great love of **adventure**.
'Alice's **Adventures** in Wonderland' is an **adventure** story for children.

Note that quite a lot of nouns have both a *countable* meaning and an *uncountable* one.

4.1.5 Plural nouns

Clothes are quite expensive here.

Some nouns exist only in the plural form and are *collective*, e.g. **clothes** (= any and all kinds of things we wear on our bodies), **goods** (= things we buy and sell). Naturally, these are followed by plural verbs, and any determiner has to be **these**, **those**, **many**, not **this**, **that**, **much**. We cannot count collective nouns, except as follows:

'Now, where did I put my glasses?'

These trousers are nice, aren't they?
– Yes, they're my best **ones**.
Have you got the **scissors**?
– **They are** already in my bag.

Some plural nouns refer to things which have two similar parts, e.g. (a pair of) **glasses** (= spectacles), (a pair of) **jeans**, (a pair of) **pyjamas**, (a pair of), **scissors**, (a pair of) **shears**, (a pair of) **trousers**. The word **pair** can be counted, e.g. three **pairs** of jeans.

People were blocking the road.
Police have driven the crowd back.

Some *group nouns*, above all **police** and **people**, are used in plural only, even though they do not end in plural **s**.

The **crowd**	was / were	whistling.
The **government**	has / have	been defeated at last.

However, the majority of *group nouns* may be treated as either singular or plural. The deciding factor is whether we want to say something about the group as a whole, or whether we want to say something about each of its members. Words in this category include **army**, **class**, **club**, **crowd**, **family**, **government**, **team**.

4.1.6 Nationality and language nouns

Country	Single citizen	The whole nation	Adjective	Language
Germany America (the USA) Italy	a German an American an Italian	the Germans the Americans the Italians	German music American cars Italian opera	German American English Italian
England Ireland Scotland Wales France	an English-man/woman 3 English-men/women an Irishman a Scotsman a Scot a Welshman a Frenchman	the English the Irish the Scots the Scottish the Welsh the French	English weather Irish whiskey Scottish wool but: Scotch whisky Welsh songs French cheese	English Irish English, Gaelic Scottish English, Gaelic Welsh French
Britain Spain	a Briton* a Spaniard a Spanish woman	the British the Spanish	a British passport Spanish wine	British English Spanish
Japan Portugal	a Japanese a Portuguese	the Japanese the Portu-guese	Japanese food Portuguese sardines	Japanese Portuguese
Greece Denmark Switzer-land	a Greek a Dane a Swiss	the Greeks the Danes the Swiss	Greek islands Danish butter Swiss banks	Greek Danish Swiss German, French, Italian

Nationality nouns ending in **an** (like **German**, **Italian** and **American**) form their plurals, as nouns usually do, by adding **s**.

Words which end in **sh/ch** (e.g. **the Dutch**) always refer to the whole nation.

To talk about an individual citizen, we have to add **man** or **woman** to this.

In the plural we can say **Dutchmen** or **Dutch people**.

In addition, the adjective form can always be used to state nationality in sentences like My penfriend is **Polish**.

The language spoken in a country is normally the adjective, written with a capital letter.

Words ending in **ese** are both noun and adjective, and are used in the same form to describe single citizens, the whole nation, and their language.

There are also a number of irregular nationality nouns and adjectives.

*In informal English you may also hear **Brit** (**a Brit**, **several Brits**).

4.2 Articles

4.2.1 The indefinite article

In English, we use the *indefinite article* with *common nouns* which we are mentioning for the first time, unless the general context makes them specific enough for us to use the definite article (see 4.2.3).

a /ə/		**an** /ən/
a man		an old man
a uniform		an umbrella /ənʌmˈbrelə/
a horse		an hour /ənaʊəʳ/
a big apple		an apple

There are two forms of the *indefinite article* in English:

a before words that begin with a consonant sound

an before words that begin with a vowel sound

Note that it is the *sound* which is the deciding factor. We use **an** before **hour** /aʊəʳ/ because the **h** is silent; and we use **a** before **uniform** because the **u** is pronounced /juː/.

When **an** is said, it is usually joined onto the following noun, e.g. **an apple** sounds like one word /əˈnæpl/.

If an adjective is placed in front of a noun, this may change the article, e.g. **an hour**, but **a golden hour**.

'He wants to become a dentist.'

John is **a** student/**a** dentist.
In his holidays he works as **a** taxi-driver.
I know Salma is **an** Arab. But is she **(a)** Muslim or **(a)** Christian?

The indefinite article is used before the complement in the pattern *S + **be** + complement*, when the complement is the name of a profession, an occupation, a nationality, or a follower of one of certain religions.

In the case of religions, the same word is often treated as either an adjective or a noun, e.g. She is Christian/Catholic. or She is a Christian/a Catholic. We have to be careful not to extend this freedom to nationalities where nouns and adjectives have different forms, e.g. He is French. but He is a Frenchman. (NEVER He is a French).

We go to school five days **a** week.
How much are these apples? – 80p **a** kilo.

The *indefinite article* has a special use in phrases which state weights or frequencies. The alternative **per** is not used much now. (We have four weeks' leave **per** annum. = We have four weeks' leave **a** year.)

He must be hungry – he's eaten half **a** loaf of bread already!
I've been waiting for half **an** hour.
What **an** adventure!
Such **a** shame!

The *indefinite article* follows the words **half**, **quite**, and exclamatory **such** and **what** when they are followed by singular nouns.

Won't you take **a seat**? – No, thanks, I'm in **a hurry**.

Note that the *indefinite article* also forms part of a number of idiomatic expressions: **have a headache**, **take a seat**, **be in a hurry** (see 4.5.16.1).

4.2.2 The zero article

By *zero article* we mean the absence of an article, principally before *countable nouns* in the plural.

A student goes to a university to get a degree.
= Students go to universities to get degrees.
Elephants have trunks.
= An elephant has a trunk.
= The elephant has a trunk.
Detective stories are my favourite reading.
I love a good detective story.
I don't like spiders, do you?

The *zero article* is used in front of plural *countable nouns* when we mean all things of this kind, e.g. all elephants. But English sometimes allows us to express the same ideas using singular nouns with appropriate articles.

When the emphasis is strongly on all members of the class, as in the last example on **spiders**, we must use the *zero article*.

Let's go **by bus**.
I'll see you **at school** tomorrow.

Zero article is also used in certain fixed expressions. (See also *proper nouns, abstract nouns*, seasons, months, days of the week, meals, under 4.2.3.)

4.2.3 The definite article

In English, we use the *definite article,* **the,** with *common nouns* which we have mentioned earlier in the same conversation, or which in some way are made specific by the general context of what we are saying. Its pronunciation is weak in front of words beginning with a consonant sound (**the bird** /ðə bɜːd/), but strong in front of words beginning with a vowel sound (**the air** /ði eəʳ/).

Ben Nevis is the highest mountain in Great Britain (1343m).
Lake Windermere is really beautiful.
We went shopping in **Oxford Street**.

---

the Netherlands, the USA (= the United States of America), the Isle of Wight, the Tower (of London), the Atlantic Ocean, the Red Sea, the United Kingdom, the North Pole, the Tropic of Cancer, the Equator.

London is near the mouth of **the Thames**.

Dinner is ready.
Summer can be rather warm in Scotland.

The dinner we had yesterday was really excellent.
The summer of 1980 was rather cool.
A dinner I once had in a Russian airport will stay in my memory for ever.

Proper nouns (names) usually do not have an article. These proper nouns include not only names of people, but also of geographical features (names of mountains, lakes, buildings, streets, etc.)

NOTES
Exceptions to the above statement are names which are plural in form (e.g. the United States) or whose principal noun is one which can have a plural, e.g. **sea** in the Red Sea.

This applies also to the names of rivers even when the word **River** is missing.

The names of seasons, months, days of the week and meals are used without an article when we talk about them in a general way.

But when we want to be more specific, and single out one from many, we have to put an *article* in front. This singling out is often done with a *relative clause* or an **of**-phrase. The article may be *definite* or *indefinite*. The choice depends on how specific we want to be, i.e. The dinner we had yesterday. is more specific than A dinner I once had in a Russian airport.

The school I go to is a very big building.
Where is **the church,** please? (= the building)
There isn't **a school** in this village.
but:
School begins at 8 o'clock.
Are you going to **church** now? (= the service)

Nouns like **school, church, hospital** can have two meanings: the building itself, and what goes on inside it, i.e. education, worship, care of the sick. If we mean the buildings, we use an article, which may again be definite or indefinite; but if we mean their work, we use zero article. (For use of articles after prepositions, e.g. **go by bus,** see 4.5.18.)

Roadside Notice:
Death is so permanent.

Abstract nouns, like **death, history, life, mankind, society,** do not have an article even when there is an adjective in front of them, e.g. **modern art, Chinese civilization.**

Modern art can be quite puzzling.

But here too an article is needed if the abstract noun is qualified by an **of**-phrase or a *relative clause*.

The history of the American West is really fascinating.
The life the gold-diggers led in the camps was very hard.

People were blocking the roads.
The people of Canada welcomed their Queen warmly.
The people outside the hall could not hear as well as those inside.
Most of **the people** in the blazing hotel were rescued by firemen.

The word **people** does not have an article, unless it is qualified by a *relative clause*, an *of*-phrase, a *prepositional phrase*, or the context. There is also no article in front of **most** when it means 'the majority of the'.

Both (the) brothers had disappeared.
All the money was gone.
Half the food in the cupboard was bad.

The *definite article* follows **all**, **both**, and **double**, though it is often omitted after **both**. The definite article also follows **half** if the noun is qualified by an *of*-phrase, a *relative clause*, or a *prepositional phrase*. (Compare *half* + *indefinite article*, in 4.2.1.)

4.3 Adjectives

4.3.1 Positions of adjectives

> The National Theatre is a **new** building.
> It's **big** and **modern.**

We place *adjectives* either in front of the nouns which they describe, or after parts of the verb **be** (see 4.3.4). The first use is called *attributive*, the second *predicative*.

English adjectives do not have different singular and plural forms; they always remain the same.

> You should see 'Hamlet' at the National Theatre.
> The production is **very interesting.**
> And the actors are **absolutely marvellous.**

Adjectives themselves can be further qualified:
- by *adverbs* such as **very, quite, rather, so**
- by *adverbs* made from adjectives by adding **ly**.

4.3.2 The adjective used as a noun

> **The Welsh** are very proud of their country.
> Even **the young** are fond of their traditional folk music.

In English we may use an adjective as a noun only when we mean something as a whole: **the poor** (= all people who do not have enough money to feed and clothe themselves properly, etc.); **the young** (= young people everywhere, the younger generation).

> In the urban areas of Wales, **the Welsh** do not often speak Welsh.

Nationality adjectives ending in **sh**, **ch**, and **ese** are also used in this way, e.g. **the English** (= all the English race or nation, at any period of their history, or at some particular time made clear by the context). (See also 4.1.6.)

Adjectives used as nouns in this way require the definite article, and are not given a plural ending (see 4.2.3).

Five **injured people** were taken to the hospital.

When we are talking about a certain number of people, not people in general, we must add to the adjective a word like **people**, **men**, **women**, **children**, **workers**, etc.

Judith took to drinking and in a few years became **an alcoholic**.
She was eventually saved by an organization which cares for fellow **drunks**, called **Alcoholics** Anonymous . . .
Jesse Jackson was **the first Black** to run as a presidential candidate in the USA.

Adjectives used as nouns may in time be regarded as countable, e.g. **a Christian**, **a Catholic** (see 4.2.1).

4.3.3 The adjective with pronoun *one*

This sweater is too expensive.
Can you show me a cheaper **one**?
Which grapes do you want?
The white **ones** or the black **ones**?

To avoid having to repeat a *countable noun* we may substitute **one** (singular) or **ones** (plural). (For **one**, see 4.5.9.)

4.3.4 Special predicative uses of adjectives

This cake **looks** really **good**.
These grapes **taste good**.
I'm **feeling fine**.
Why does she **seem** so **sad**, I wonder?

There is a group of verbs which we use to talk about the appearance of things, or how our senses react to them in other ways: **appear**, **feel**, **look**, **seem**, **smell**, **sound**, **taste**. These verbs do not describe actions, but states, and are followed by an *adjective* (NOT an adverb).

Tom is **ill**, he can't come.
But you look quite **well** again now.

A number of adjectives can be used only as *predicates* (i.e. after **be**) and never attributively (i.e. in front of nouns). In particular, this group includes adjectives which describe our state of health.

something looks good (= is attractive to the eye)
somebody looks well (= looks healthy)

4.3.5 Comparison of adjectives

Positive (*base*)	Comparative	Superlative
Many houses with brick walls are **old**. Glasgow is **big**. This bag is **heavy**.	Houses with wooden frames are usually **older**. London is **bigger**. This suitcase is **heavier**.	Houses with simple mud walls are **oldest**. New York is **biggest**. This box is **heaviest**.
Hockey is **popular**. Cars with four gears are **common**.	Cricket is **more popular**. Cars with five gears are **less common**.	**Football is most** popular. Cars with only three gears are **least common**.

Many adjectives form their *comparatives* and *superlatives* by adding **er** and **est** to the *base*. This applies to adjectives of one syllable, as well as adjectives of two syllables ending in **er, le, ow, y** (e.g. **clever, gentle, narrow, heavy**).

Please notice that, before **er/est**, final consonants are doubled after a stressed vowel written as a single letter; and that **y** changes to **i**.

The comparative of all remaining adjectives is formed by putting the adverb **more** in front of the adjective, and the superlative by putting the adverb **most** in front. This applies to all adjectives with three or more syllables, and those with two syllables which do not end in **er, le, ow, y**.

With **more** and **most** we can compare things on an increasing scale. We can also compare on a decreasing scale, using **less** and **least**.

The Angel Falls in Venezuela are **the tallest in the world**.   Many snakes are poisonous, but the king cobra is probably **the most dangerous of them all**.

When a following phrase or the context requires it, *a definite article* is added to the *superlative*.

Positive	Comparative	Superlative
good **bad**	**better** **worse**	**best** **worst**

There are a few adjectives which have irregular comparatives.

We shall spend **little** time in Wells, and (even) **less** time in Glastonbury.   John is rather a **little** boy for his age, but he isn't **the smallest** boy in his class.

We use the comparative and superlative forms of **little** to talk about quantities only, i.e. with uncountable nouns. If we want to compare sizes (i.e. of countable nouns) we use **smaller** – **smallest** instead of **less** – **least**.

near	nearer	nearest
		next

The **nearest** station is Charing Cross.
The **next** stop is at Charing Cross. (But we pass through three other stations on the way.)

A few adjectives have more than one comparative or superlative form, but these usually have slightly different meanings. An example is:
nearest (= in *distance*), **next** (= in *sequence*).

'*Yes, sir. This is the Norwegian frontier.*
But the first Norwegian town is farther down the road. It's about ten kilometres, and there's no bus!'

This tree belongs to me, but the **farther** one is in my neighbour's garden.
Have you any **further** questions?

Far also has two comparative forms:
farther/'fɑːðə/ is used only to compare *distances*.
further/'fɜːðə/ is also used to compare *distances*, but has a second meaning, 'additional'.

The last news of Smith was that he had reached the North Pole. He was never heard of again.
The latest report says several people died in the crash. We hope to give you the exact number and names in our next bulletin.

Late has the superlative **last** (= final) and **latest** (= most recent, i.e. the last so far, but we expect more later).
Old has the comparative and superlative forms **older, oldest,** which we use generally to compare ages, e.g. Britain has the **oldest** parliament in the world. But we use the forms **elder, eldest,** to describe family relationships only, e.g. **my elder brother/my eldest sister/their eldest child**. Note that you should only use **elder, eldest**, in front of nouns, i.e. attributively.

> This box is **much heavier** (than that one).
> This tune is **slightly more difficult** to play.

Comparatives of adjectives can be further qualified by adverbs such as **much, slightly**.

4.3.6 Degrees of comparison

> Wales is **as interesting as** Scotland.
> Holiday camps are **cheaper than** hotels.
> They can be **more exciting than** hotels, too.
>
> But then again, youth hostels are **not so expensive as** holiday camps.
> (= They are **less** expensive **than** holiday camps.)

Three *degrees of comparison* are possible:
– we can say things are equal: to do this we use *as Adj* **as**.
– we can say things are higher on a scale: to do this we use *Adj+**er than*** or ***more** Adj **than***.
– we can say things are lower on a scale: to do this we use ***not so** Adj **as, not as** Adj **as** or **less** Adj **than*** (see 2.3.4 and 2.3.5).

4.4 Adverbs

4.4.1 Forms of adverbs

> Both teams began **nervously**.
> Francis tricked one man **beautifully** and put his team in the lead.
> But Arsenal fought back **fantastically**.
> They won the match **easily** by 4-1.
> Nottingham manager Clough was **terribly** disappointed.

Most English adverbs are different from the corresponding adjectives in form. The majority are in fact derived from adjectives by adding **ly**.

In the process, adjectives ending in **y** after a consonant change to **i: easy → easily**. And the ending **le** disappears if it follows a consonant: **terrible → terribly**.

From adjectives ending in **ic** we derive adverbs ending in **ally,** e.g. **scientifically**. But note the exception **publicly**.

He was treated in **a friendly way**.

Note that because the adjective **friendly** already ends in **ly**, it would sound ugly if we added a further **ly** to make an adverb. We avoid this by using the expression **in a friendly way**.

He has got a **fast** car. → He drove too **fast**.
She is a **hard** worker. → She works **hard**.

Some adverbs have the same form as the corresponding adjective. The most important of these are **farther**, **fast**, **further**, **hard**, **more**, **most**.

Could you speak up a bit? I can **hardly** understand you.

Try not to confuse **hard** with **hardly**, which means 'barely' (i.e. 'nearly not').

Our teacher **seemed** quite **calm** at first.
But suddenly he **became/got** very **angry**.
He **grew pale** and then **turned red** again and began to shout ...

An adjective is also found after verbs which refer to a present or future state, such as **be**, **seem**, **become**, **get** (= become), **turn** (= change to being).

He **looked furious**. → He **looked at** us **furiously**.

(For more about adjectives and adverbs after **feel** and **look**, see 4.3.4.)

Do you like adventure stories?
– Very much so, and I like science fiction, { **as well**. **too**.
Could you lend me one?
– Of course, you can have something by Jules Verne. But you can **also** have H. G. Wells's 'The War of the Worlds'.
Oh, did you see the film the other day?
– I didn't, unfortunately.
– I didn't see it, **either**.

too/as well/also/either:
These four adverbs enable us to add ideas to ones that have been previously expressed.
   As well and **too** appear at the ends of sentences, often separated from the other words by a comma. **Also**, which has exactly the same meaning, is usually placed in *medial position* (see 1.1.12). In negative sentences, **either** is used instead of **too** (see 1.4.7).

She's **good** at playing the piano. → She plays very **well**.

The adverb corresponding to **good** is **well**.

4.4.2 Comparison of adverbs

> Private cars are a problem in this city.
> Their owners **more frequently** leave them in their driveways than in a garage.
> But **most commonly** of all, they simply park them in the streets.

Adverbs ending in **ly** form their comparative with **more** and their superlative with **most**.

> He spoke **faster** than I was used to.
> And he left much **earlier** than his sister.
> He travelled **farther** south than any man had ever been before.

If an adverb is exactly the same as the corresponding adjective, it forms its comparative and superlative in the same way, too.

Irregular comparatives:

well	better	best
badly	worse	worst

4.4.3 Kinds of adverbs and their meanings

As the name suggests, adverbs serve to modify (that is, to give use more exact information about)
– verbs especially;
– but also adjectives;
– other adverbs;
– and finally, whole sentences.

> I was sitting in my room and **reading quietly**.
> The book was **extremely interesting**.
> I went to bed **rather late**.
> **Suddenly** I heard a noise in the attic.
> **Frankly**, I was scared to death.

Depending on their functions in sentences, we can divide them into several categories:
– *adverbs of place and time*, like **inside**, **yesterday**;
– *adverbs of frequency*, like **frequently**, **never**, **often**, **sometimes**;
– *adverbs of degree*, like **quite**, **rather**, **very**, which strengthen or weaken adjectives or other adverbs;
– *adverbs of manner*, like **quietly**, **nervously**, **fast**, which tell us how something happened;

– *sentence adverbials*, like **frankly**, **unfortunately**, which modify a sentence in its entirety.

(For the positions of these different kinds of adverbs in the sentence, see 1.1.11 to 1.1.15.)

We use **still** in questions as well as statements, when we wish to say that something is/was taking longer than we expect(ed) (see 1.4.5).

Yet, at the end of a sentence, is used if we wish to find out if there has been an unexpected delay to prevent something happening, and to give negative answers to questions of that kind (see 1.4.5 again).

Why, **when** and **where** are used to begin *restrictive* and *non-restrictive clauses* and are then called *relative adverbs*. Notice that they have the same meaning as a relative pronoun + a preposition, and that the preposition disappears when the *relative adverb* is used (see 2.3.1).

> Are you **still** here – Yes, I **still** have some work to do.
> Has John come **yet**? – No, he hasn't come **yet**.
> Wait a moment. The water is not boiling **yet**.

> I don't know the reason **why** she's always silent.
> Christmas is the time **when** our whole family gets together.
> (Christmas is the time **at which** …)
> We had our holiday in Spain, **where** the weather's always warm at that time of year.

4.5 Pronouns and quantifiers

4.5.1 Personal pronouns

Subject form	I	you	he	she	it	we	you	they
Object form	me	you	him	her	it	us	you	them

In English, *personal pronouns* have only two forms: when they are used as *subjects*, and when they are used as *objects*.

> He likes **her** very much.
> He gave **her** a present.

A single *object form* is used for both direct and indirect objects.

> Who's that? – It's **me**.

Even after the verb **be**, it is mostly the *object form* which is used (see 2.3.5).

> **You** can't have your cake and eat it. (*English proverb*) (One can't have one's . . .)
> **They**
> **People** } say the British prefer plain cooking.

You is more often used than **one**, with the same sense; and **they** is as common as **people**, again with the same sense (see 1.1.8).

> What's your new **teacher** like?
> – Oh, **she's** all right. **She** doesn't make a fuss when we forget our homework.

A **doctor**, **teacher**, **writer**, etc. is called **he** or **she**, depending on his or her sex. The same applies to **baby** and **friend**.

> **Germany** has always been proud of **her** composers.
> The Titanic was supposed to be a safe ship, but **she** sank on her maiden voyage.

Note that countries, ships and cars may also be referred to as **she** and **her**.

> Where's the sausage? Have you taken **it?**
> What's the matter with your leg? – **It's** broken.
> What kind of dog have you got? – **It's/He's** a sheepdog.

The pronouns **he** and **she** are normally used for human beings and **it** for everything else.
   But if we have a personal relationship with an animal (e.g. it is a pet in our house), we may call if **he** or **she**; otherwise we use **it**.

4.5.2 Special uses of *it*

> He's 105. – I don't believe **it**!
> Do we need our umbrellas? – I don't think **so**.
> Will he come? – Well, at least he said **so**.

In some English sentences, **it** has the meaning 'what you have just said'. But in others, the word **so** must be used instead.

We can also use **it** for special emphasis (see 2.3.14).

It's no $\left\{ \begin{array}{l} \textbf{use} \\ \textbf{good} \end{array} \right\}$ crying over spilt milk.

It's (not) worth trying again.

It replaces the normal subject in expressions like **It's no use, It's no good, It's (not) worth**. Notice these expressions are usually followed by **ing** forms (see 4.1.3).

4.5.3 Possessive pronouns

There are two different types of *possessive pronouns – attributive* possessive pronouns, which function like adjectives, and which are placed before a noun in a sentence; and *substantive* (also called *predicative*) possessive pronouns, which function like nouns, and which may appear in a sentence either in the position of subject, or as object or complement after the verb.

4.5.3.1 Adjective-like possessive pronouns

I must get	**my**	bike.
Have you repaired	**your**	bike?
He cleans	**his**	bike once a week.
She likes	**her**	pet.
It's a hamster and	**its**	name is Jerry.
We must do	**our**	homework.
Have you done	**your**	homework, Tom and Mary?
They're proud of	**their**	skates.

Note the correct spelling of the possessive pronoun for things in the singular, **its,** and don't confuse it with **it's** (the shortened form of **it is**).

Please take **your** cap off.
Tim broke **his** leg.

Adjective-like possessive pronouns are used in English where some other languages would use the *definite article* instead. In English, we should understand Tim broke the leg to mean he broke the leg of a chair, or a chicken, perhaps, which had been mentioned earlier.

Many drivers risk **their lives** by not wearing their safety belts.

When we talk about things which are true of all people or many people, the plural possessive pronoun **their** is often used with nouns like **lives, minds**.

I've got **my own** room.
Have you got a room **of your own?**

We can emphasize adjective-like possessive pronouns by adding the word **own**. (Note that in some languages, a word with the same meaning as **own** can follow the definite or indefinite article. This is not possible in English.)

4.5.3.2 Noun-like possessive pronouns

My birthday is on the 29th of February.
And when is **yours?**
– Oh, **mine** is on the 1st of April.

Noun-like possessive pronouns are used when we want to avoid repeating a noun already used earlier in the same sentence, or in the previous sentence.

With the one exception of **his**, they are all different in form from the adjective-like possessive pronouns.

There is no noun-like possessive pronoun equivalent to **its**.

Possessive pronouns	
Adjective-like	Noun-like
my	**mine**
your (s & pl)	**yours** (s & pl)
his	**his**
her	**hers**
its	–
our	**ours**
their	**theirs**

Who's that girl over there?
– Linda? Oh, she's an old friend/a cousin/an employee **of mine.**
You're not going to take me on another holiday in that terrible old car **of yours!**

Sometimes the noun-like possessive pronoun is used in an *of*-phrase (see 4.1.2): an employee of mine = one of my employees.

4.5.4 Pronouns ending in *self* or *selves*

Singular	Plural
myself	**ourselves**
yourself	**yourselves**
herself	
himself	**themselves**
itself	

'Do it yourself.'

The endings of these pronouns are **self** in the singular and **selves** in the plural. The first part is usually the same as the *adjective-like possessive pronoun*, but note **him** (not **his**) and **them** (not **their**). Also **itself** is spelt with only one **s**.

These pronouns are used in two ways:
– for *emphasis* (when used in this way some grammar books call them 'intensifiers');
– as *reflexive pronouns*.

The headmaster **himself** said so./The headmaster said so **himself**.
You can ask him **yourself**.
You can ask the headmaster **himself**.
We did it **ourselves**.

May I introduce **myself?** My name is Wolf.
Nice to meet you. I hope you'll enjoy **yourself**.

If you work for two companies, you may work **against yourself**.
The pupils wrote **about themselves**.

These examples are of pronouns ending in **self** or **selves** which have been used for *emphasis*.

Notice that their position in the sentence is after the noun which they emphasize; but if we want to emphasize the subject of the sentence, and the sentence itself is fairly short, the pronoun may come at the end.

As *reflexive pronouns*, pronouns ending in **self** and **selves** are used when we want to say that the subject of the sentence does (did/has done, etc.) something to itself.

Reflexive pronouns may also follow a preposition.

PEANUTS

English Essay
"What I Did This Summer"

9-15

I played ball, and I went to camp.

ONE, TWO, THREE, FOUR, FIVE, SIX, SEVEN, EIGHT....

NINE HUNDRED AND NINETY-TWO WORDS TO GO!

SCHULZ

'He's writing about himself.'

In the morning I **wash, brush** my teeth, and **dress** quickly. Then I . . .

English uses reflexive pronouns less often than some other languages. They are not used if it is clear from the context that the verb describes an action which the subject does to itself.

4.5.5 Reciprocal pronouns: *each other/one another*

Alan and David always help	each other. one another.

We can say that A does/did something to B, and B does/did the same to A, by using the *reciprocal pronouns* **each other** or **one another**. (As you will see from the example, we can use the two reciprocal pronouns in exactly the same way.)

The two girls are looking at **themselves**.

These two examples show the difference between the meaning of a *reflexive pronoun* and that of a *reciprocal pronoun*.

The two girls are looking at	each other. one another.

4.5.6 Demonstrative pronouns

this book (here)   **that** man (there) **these** men (here) **those** books (there)

We refer to people and things using the same pronouns: **this** and **that** are singular, and **these** and **those** are plural.

Do you know **that** man over there?
I was just beginning to climb down **those** cliffs (over there).
At **that** moment I heard somebody cry for help.
I don't like **that** sort of person.

We use **that/those** when we want to show that there is a gap, in space or time (sometimes even a distance in feeling), between ourselves and the person or thing we are discussing.

On the telephone:
Who's **that** speaking? (BrE)
Who is **this**? (AmE)

Note, however, a difference in BrE and AmE usage when asking about the identity of a caller on the telephone.

Which T-shirt do you want?
This one or **that** one?
This one's cheap but **that** one's dearer.
I'd prefer one of **those** (green ones).

This and **that** (or **these** and **those**) may be used with objects which are the same distance away, if we want to compare or contrast them, or invite someone to make a selection, etc. In these circumstances, **this**, **that**, **these** and **those** may be used on their own, without a following noun.

What's { **this**? } – Our new pet, darling.
{ **that**? }

In some situations, it does not matter much whether we use **this** or **that** (**these** or **those**). But there is often a difference in feeling: use of **this/these** suggests that we are willing to accept something; conversely, **that/those** suggest rejection or at least some reservation. (The man in the cartoon would be more likely to say 'What's **that**?')

This } is what I said all the time.
That }

This is the way you can do it …

Note that **this** and **that** may also be used to connect together our remarks in a conversation. With both **this** and **that** we can refer to something we have already said. If we want to alert our listeners to something we are going to say, we use **this**.

4.5.7 Relative pronouns

who/that	– used to refer to persons
which/that	– used to refer to things
whose	– used to refer to possessions of persons and things
whom	– object form of **who**

For rules and ways of use, see the section on *relative clauses* (2.3.1).

4.5.8 *Wh*-question pronouns and other question words

The *relative pronouns* in 4.5.7 may also be used in **Wh**-question words, along with a number of other question words: **what**, **when**, **where**, **how**, etc. (For the use of these, see 1.2.6 and 1.2.7.)

Oh, you've got a new girlfriend!
What's her name?
What does she look like?
What is she like?
What about ⎱ inviting her to our party?
How about ⎰
How is she coming – by bus or by car?
Whose sister did you say she was?

Notice in particular the examples which contain **What ... like**? In some other languages, these questions would begin with a word which means **How**? i.e. the same word which is used to translate **How** in **How** is she coming? In English, How is she? has quite a different meaning from What is she like? The first is a question about her health or state of mind at this particular moment; the second about her character (or appearance) in general.

What's ⎱	the score?
How's ⎰	
What's ⎱	the time?
How's ⎰	

You may notice some occasions when either **What**? or **How**? seems to be correct. In these circumstances you will find it is safer to prefer **What**?

Where is your school?
Where are you going?
When must you leave?

We use **Where**? to ask about *place* or *direction*.
And we use **When**? to ask about *time*.

Why are you late?
How do you get to school?
How long does it take you?
How many pupils are in your class?

We use **Why**? to enquire about *reasons* or *causes*.
• And we use **How**? to ask about *manner* or *means*.

4.5.9 The pronoun *one*

Do you need a big box or just a small **one**?
– A small **one** will do.
What about these red apples?
– No, I'd rather have those green **ones**.

To avoid repeating the name of something or someone, we can use *Adj* + **one** (in the plural: *Adj* + **ones**).

(In some languages it is possible to use the adjective on its own, without **one** or **ones**, but we rarely do this in English.)

Which one of the girls is Linda?
– The **one** with the pink dress.
I do not know the other **ones**/the **others**.

If we are avoiding repetition of a noun which requires a definte article in front of it, we must put the definite article before **one** (or **ones**) instead.

Note that **other** is an exception to the previously stated rules that adjectives cannot be used on their own, or have a plural form (the **others** = the **other ones**).

Which one do you want? **This one** or **that one**?
– I think I'll take **this one**.

One and **ones** are often used after the question word **Which**? and also after *demonstrative pronouns* (see 4.5.6).

4.5.10 *Some, any* and their compounds

4.5.10.1 *Some* and *any*

What's in the fridge?
– Well, there's **some** butter. And we've also got **some** eggs.

Some and **any** tell us about quantity, but the information they give is imprecise. They may appear in front of *uncountable nouns* for commodities, such as **butter**, **bread**, as well as in front of plural *countable nouns* for things and persons, such as **eggs**, **bottles** and **policemen**. They are usually unstressed words, and the pronunciation of **some** is accordingly weak: /səm/.

I'd like some butter. Is there **any**?
– Yes, there's **some** in the fridge.

Is there **any** bread left?
– No, there isn't (**any**).
And we haven't got **any** tomatoes either.
(See also 4.5.11 for alternative use of **no**.)

There's **hardly any** milk left.
If we had **any** milk we could eat these cornflakes.

'*The computer broke down. Is there anyone here who has any experience in thinking?*'

Is there **some** tea left? (If so, I'd like some.)
Can I have **some** more tea, please?
– Certainly. Would you also like **some** biscuits?
– No, thank you. I don't want **any** now.

You can take **any** record (that) you like.
You'll get these records **anywhere**.

Some and **any** can also be used as subjects or objects, like the *noun-like possessive pronouns* (see 4.5.3.2). In this case, **some** is pronounced /sʌm/.

Some is used in positive statements (but see the exception below).

Any is used in negative statements and in questions (but once again see the exception below).

Note that **any** sometimes combines with restricting adverbs, like **hardly**, and is often found in *conditional clauses*.

Some is used in sentences which look and sound like questions, but are in fact polite *requests* for something which is known to be available, or *offers* of the same.

Any can also be used in positive statements, when it is stressed and means 'whichever'. In this use the sentence usually ends with a relative clause containing one of these verbs: **choose, like, fancy, prefer, wish, want,** e.g. (that) you like.

Similarly, words which include **any**, such as **anywhere, anyone, anybody**, may also be used in positive statements.

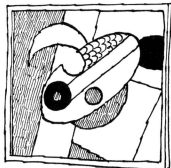

'Some say it's a picture of a fish,
but others say it's a guitar.'

Some like classical music, **others** prefer pop music.

Some also has a stressed use (pronounced /sʌm/, when its meaning is 'certain people'. It is often employed in contrastive statements: Some do this, and some (others) do that. (See also 4.5.6 for the use of **this** and **that** in contrastive statements.)

4.5.10.2 Compounds with *some* and *any*

There's **somebody** on the telephone for you.
I don't know **anybody** here.

The most important compounds with **some** and **any** are:
somebody/someone (both have the same meaning) and **anybody/anyone** (same meaning again).
These are used to talk about people, and are used exclusively as pronouns.

We need **something** (cold) to drink.
Is there **anything** left in the fridge?

We use **something/anything** to talk about things.

The bottle opener must be **somewhere** in the kitchen. But I can't find it **anywhere**.

We use **somewhere/anywhere** to talk about place or position.
As with **some/any** (see 4.5.10.1), **some**-compounds are used in positive statements, **any**-compounds in negative statements, and the same general rules apply.

Compounds of **some** and **any** can combine with **else**.

Please show me **something** else.
Let's look **somewhere** else.
Do you know **anyone else** who can speak Chinese?

117

4.5.11 *No* and its compounds

There's **no** money left. (= There isn't any money left.)
And we have **no** traveller's cheques. (= We don't have any ...)

No has the same meaning as **not any** and may be used with both *countable* and *uncountable* nouns.

No tends to sound more emphatic; for this reason, **not any** is more common.

Is there any milk left? – No, there isn't any.
– No, there's **none**.

No can only be used attributively, i.e. like an adjective before a noun. In other words, we can't use **no** to make an alternative to **There isn't any**. We have to use **none** instead.

Nobody loves me!
There's { **nobody** / **no one** } in the office now.

On the other hand, the compounds of **no** can only be used in noun position. **Nobody** and **no one** are for persons. (Note that **no one** is written as two words.)

You can do **nothing.** (= You can't do anything.)
Nowhere in the world is as good as home.

Nothing refers to things.
Nowhere (= not ... anywhere) refers to places.

There was **nowhere else** to go, so we stayed where we were.
John's Ford was in the garage, and **no one else** had a car.

Compounds of **no**, like compounds of **some** and **any** (see 4.5.10.2), may be followed by **else**.

Lady of the house: Are you enjoying yourself, Mr Wilde?
Oscar Wilde: Yes, I am. There is **nothing else** here to enjoy.

None of these old maps is/are of any use.
Which of these maps would you like? – **None** (of them).
Seven people had been invited, but **none** came.
None of this food is worth eating.

None may be used instead of **no one** for persons, and instead of **not any** for things. It is usually followed by an *of-phrase*, but can stand on its own. (See above: **There's none.** = 'There isn't any.')

If the *of*-phrase contains a *plural countable noun*, the following verb may be plural in sympathy with the noun, or singular, to agree with **none**.

4.5.12 *Every* and its compounds/*each*

He says he has a bad cold and misses work **every time** there's a big football match.

We go on an outing { **every** / **each** } term.

Every is followed by a singular noun, but has the same meaning as **all** + plural noun. (**every time** in the example = 'at all times when, whenever').

Each member of the party had brought his own camera.
There are ten of us, and twenty oranges, so there are two **each**.

Each means every one of a particular number.

When we use **each**, we tend to look at things separately, and when we use **every**, we tend to look at them as a collection. But **each** and **every** are often interchangeable.

However, **every** can only be used *attributively*, whereas **each** can be used both like an adjective and a noun.

Each of you will need a ticket.
How much are the tickets? – Two dollars **each**.

Furthermore, **each** can be followed by an *of-phrase*, but **every** can't. And we can use **each** in expressions like Two dollars **each**, but we can't use **every** in this way.

Is { **everybody** / **everyone** } ready to start?
OK. I think we've got **everything** now.
He sold **everything**.

Everybody (or **everyone**) for persons, and **everything** for things, are only used like nouns.

Jack was late, but **everybody else** was on time.
He missed the first part of the show, but saw **everything else**.

Compounds of **every**, like those of **some**, **any** and **no**, may be followed by **else**.

4.5.13 *All*

All deciduous trees lose their leaves in autumn.

When **all** is used in front of a plural noun and without an article, it really does mean *all* those in existence, without exception. The meaning is close to that of **every**.

All (of) the pupils in this class have interesting hobbies.

But when **all + (of) + the** is used with a plural noun, the reference is to a limited group, specified in the same sentence or in the general context.

Tom spends **nearly all** his pocket money on minerals.   He has collected a lot of stones and fossils and he knows **all** of them/them **all** by name.

The field of reference may be narrowed by a word in front of **all**, such as **nearly, almost. All** in front of uncountable nouns means 'the whole of'. In front of countable nouns it means 'every one of'.

He wants to learn $\left\{ \begin{array}{c} \textbf{everything} \\ \textbf{(all)} \end{array} \right\}$ about minerals.   Tell me **all** about your holiday.

Both **all** and **everything** can serve as the subjects and objects of sentences, but it is safer to use **everything**, as **all** may sound old-fashioned or rather poetic.

4.5.14 *Much/many/a lot of/plenty of/enough/several*

Let's make some fruit salad for our party.   How **much** sugar have we got?   I'm afraid we haven't got **much**.

Much and **many** are used mainly in questions and negative statements. However, use of **much** is confined to *uncountable nouns*, such as **sugar,**

How **many** oranges do we need?
I don't think we need very **many**.

Oh, you've taken **too much** salt.
So much salt isn't good for you.
Sorry, but I have **so many** (**too many**) jobs to do.

We have **many** friends in Italy.

We'll need { **a lot of** / **plenty of** } bread.

We've still got { **a lot of** / **plenty of** / **lots of** / **enough** } crisps.

Have we got **enough** bread?
– Yes, there are **several** slices. There's **enough** for the two of us.

money, **time, news**; while **many** is
confined to *countable nouns* in the
plural only, such as **oranges, boys,
people**.

NOTES
To a certain extent, **much** and **many**
are also used in positive statements,
especially if they have **so** and **too** in
front of them. In fact, in positive
statements **much** and **many** often
sound unnatural if they don't have **so**
or **too** in front of them.

For the present, therefore, the best
advice is not to use **much** and **many**
on their own in positive statements.

Positive statements with **much** or
many may be part of comparisons,
e.g. We have **many** friends in Italy,
but we have **more** in Spain. (i.e.
more than the many in Italy). The
superlative of **much** and **many** is
most (see 4.3.5).

The expressions used most
commonly in positive statements in
preference to **much** and **many** are **a
lot of** and **plenty of**. In spoken
English especially, **lots of** is heard
as an alternative to **a lot of**.

We can use **enough** with both
countable and *uncountable nouns*,
but **several** is used with *countable
nouns* only.

'Take your time over the next move.
We've got lots of time

4.5.15 *A little/a few; little/few*

Do you take milk in your tea?
– Just **a little**.

We've only got **a few** bottles of Coke.

I haven**'t** got **much** time.

Can you let me have some flour?
– Yes, I've got **a little** I can give you.
– No, sorry. I've got (only a) **little** for myself.
How's your fruit harvest this year?
– Quite good. We've got a lot of plums and **a few** apples, too.
– Terrible! There are **few** plums and no apples at all.

We use **a little** with *uncountable nouns*. More often than not, **just** or **only** appears in front of **a little**.

On the other hand, **a few** is used with the plural forms of *countable nouns*. If we wish to talk about a very small quantity of some commodity, or a very small number of some items, we very often use the expressions **not much** and **not many**, respectively.

A little or **little**? **A few** or **few**?
The difference between **a little** and **little**, also **a few** and **few**, is often one of viewpoint.

If we want to emphasize that we have some, even though not much, we use **a little**. If we want to emphasize that we have some, even though not many, we use **a few**. In other words, the statement is essentially positive.

But if we want to emphasize that we haven't got enough, we prefer **little** for uncountable nouns, and **few** for countable ones. **Little** usually means **only a little, too little**, therefore, and **few** usually means **only a few, too few**. In other words, they are essentially negative.

4.5.16 Numbers

4.5.16.1 Cardinal numbers

0 nought/zero		
1 one	11 eleven	21 twenty-one
2 two	12 twelve	22 twenty-two
3 three	13 thirteen	30 thirty
4 four	14 fourteen	40 forty
5 five	15 fifteen	50 fifty
6 six	16 sixteen	60 sixty
7 seven	17 seventeen	70 seventy
8 eight	18 eighteen	80 eighty
9 nine	19 nineteen	90 ninety
10 ten	20 twenty	100 a/one hundred
		101 a/one hundred and one
		200 two hundred
		1,000 one (a) thousand
		5,678 five thousand six
		5,678 hundred and seventy-
		5,678 eight
		100,000 one hundred thousand
		1,000,000 one million

There are several different ways of saying **0**. The commonest, which we use when counting and reading numbers, is **nought** /nɔːt/.

On scales, e.g. of temperature, we say **zero** /'zɪərəʊ/. When we give someone a telephone number, we say **0** /əʊ/. In football scores there is also **nil** /nɪl/, e.g. Liverpool 1 (one), Manchester United 0 (nil); and in tennis scores **love**, e.g. forty-love.

Unless it is emphasized, the number **one** is replaced by the indefinite article **a(n)**, e.g. I can see a cow ... no, two cows, three cows ...

Punctuation:
The British system is to use a comma to divide thousands from hundreds, and millions from thousands, e.g. The population of the United Kingdom was 55,583,000 in 1979. (No comma is used in dates.) A full stop is used to show decimals, e.g. Pi equals 3.14159.

8 million inhabitants: like **hundred** and **thousand**, we only add plural **s** when there is no figure in front, e.g. millions of seabirds.

Further peculiarities:
thirty-four: a hyphen is placed between tens and units.
four, fourteen, forty: **ou** changes to **o**, though pronunciation does not alter.
five, fifteen, fifty: **v** becomes **f** and the silent **e** disappears. Pronunciation changes, i.e. **five** /faɪv/, but **fifty** /'fɪfti/.

4.5.16.2 Ordinal numbers

1st first	11th eleventh
2nd second	12th twelfth
3rd third	13th thirteenth
4th fourth	
5th fifth	20th twentieth
6th sixth	21st twenty-first
7th seventh	
8th eighth	
9th ninth	33rd thirty-third
10th tenth	
	100th one-hundredth
	1000th one-thousandth

Almost all *ordinal numbers* are formed by adding **th** to the equivalent *cardinal number*.

The exceptions which are most different are the first three numbers: **first**, **second**, **third**, which afterwards reappear in combinations like **twenty-first**, **thirty-second**, **forty-third**, etc. But notice also these differences in spelling: **eighth**, **ninth**, **twentieth**, **thirtieth**, etc.; and these differences in both spelling and pronunciation: **fifth** (/fɪfθ;) twelfth (/twelfθ/).

In writing, the full form, e.g. **seventh**, is used in sentences, but in dates, lists of winners, etc. shortened forms are used, e.g. **(Monday) 7th July**. In America, **July 7** is the common written form (see 4.5.17).

Names of kings and queens: Roman numerals are used, e.g. **Richard III**. This is read **Richard the Third**.

I can't come to the fair with you.
Firstly, I haven't got any money.
Secondly, I've already got another date.

We use *ordinal numbers* to show a sequence of people, days, etc. If we wish to sequence points in an argument, we may use an adverb form of the same ordinal numbers, i.e. **firstly**, **secondly**, **thirdly**.

4.5.16.3 Expressions of frequency

I go to the pictures	**once a month**.
I play football	**twice a week**.
I clean my teeth	**three times a day**.
I phone my girlfriend at least	**six times a day**.

Once (= one time), **twice** (= two times). Beyond **twice** we add *time* to the *cardinal number*.

4.5.16.4 Fractions and decimals

½ = (one) half;
⅔ = two thirds;
¾ = three quarters;
5³⁄₁₀ = five and three tenths

0.5 = { nought point five / point five

1.33 = one point three three

4.5.17 Time of day and dates

The clock is divided mentally into two halves: for the first thirty minutes after the hour we look back, and say **past**, e.g. **ten past two**. This includes the half hour itself, e.g. **half past nine**. For the next 29 minutes we look forward, and say **to**, e.g. **twenty-nine minutes to seven, (a) quarter to six**. The hour itself is started by saying the word **o'clock**, although in conversation this is often omitted when the meaning is clear without it, e.g. Time for supper! **It's eight** (**o'clock**).

We can leave out the word **minutes** if the number in front of it is a multiple of 5, but not if it is a number like 18 or 23.

When it is necessary to distinguish morning times from afternoon and evening ones, phrases like **in the evening** are used in speech, and the abbreviations **a.m.** and **p.m.** in writing, i.e. **10.00 p.m.** = ten o'clock at night.

The twenty-four hour clock is being used more and more these days. **9.35** is read (**at**) **nine thirty-five** and **18.00** is read (**at**) **eighteen hundred hours**.

Modern digital display:

16:04

Ways of writing dates:

2nd January/2 January 1939
January 2nd/January 2, 1939
2/1/1939 – 2.1.39 (in Britain) = 1/2/1939 – 1.2.39 (in USA)

Pronunciations:

the second of January nineteen (hundred and) thirty-nine.
January the second, nineteen (hundred and) thirty-nine.
(see 5.3)

NOTES
In the USA the sequence **January 2, 1939** is preferred. If dates are given in figures only, it is important to know whether the writer is American or British, because **1.2.1984** = **1st February 1984** in Britain, but **January 2, 1984** in the USA.

4.5.18 Prepositions

4.5.18.1 Prepositions of place and direction

In the picture you can see:

1 – a woman going **into** the supermarket to do her shopping, and a man coming **out of** the supermarket. He is carrying two bags **of** shopping.

2 – a girl walking **across** the road. She is going **to** the supermarket, too.

3 – some people getting **off** the bus. A young man is waiting to get **on** the bus.

4 – someone looking **out of** the bus window.

5 – some children running **along** the street. The girl is running **after/behind** the boy.

6 – a women with a pram walking **past*** the supermarket.

7 – a man and woman walking **towards** the bus.

8 – another man walking **away from** the bus.

9 – a woman walking **through** the door of the café. Her child is pointing **to/towards/in the direction of** the bus.

10 – a man walking **round** the corner **from** the car park.

11 – a woman going **up** the steps **into** the library. A man is coming **down** the steps **from** the library with some books.

12 – a café **next to** a greengrocer's. The greengrocer's is **between** the café and the bank.

* Note the spelling. The preposition **past** is often confused with the past tense verb **passed**.

13 – a greengrocer's with a 'For Sale' notice on the wall **above/over** the door.

14 – a bank **near** the café.

15 – a boy and a girl **inside** the café having a cup of coffee. They have left their bicycles **outside** the café.

16 – a car waiting **at** the pedestrian crossing. A man is sitting **in** the car and you can see some people **on** the bus.

17 – a boy **on** a bicycle **behind** the car.

18 – some people crossing the road **in front of** the car. The child is walking **beside/at the side of** the man.

19 – a bus stop·**opposite** the supermarket.

20 – a bank with people waiting **by** the door for it to open.

21 – a man leaning **against** the wall of the bank **below/under/beneath/underneath** the sign.

22 – There are some cabbages **among** the vegetables on the stall outside the greengrocer's.

4.5.18.2 **Prepositions of time**

At 8 o'clock, **at** noon, **at** that moment,
at the weekend, **at** Christmas, **at** Easter
In 1985, **in** spring, **in** May,
In the morning, afternoon, evening

On Friday, **on** January 2nd, **on** the following day
Till Monday, **until** Christmas, **till** 12 o'clock

At, in, on, until:

at	with points or moments in time, including festivals
in	with years, seasons, months and most periods of the day
on	with days of the week
till	} with any of the above
until	

Since, for:

since	measuring the time forwards from an event or time (see 3.4.2.3).
for	with periods of time – stating the duration of an activity (see 3.4.2.3).

Since 2 o'clock, **since** Monday, **since** 1984
I've been here **for** 2 hours, 3 weeks, 1 year.
We'll stay there **for** 3 weeks.

We can start **after** breakfast, but must be back **before** lunchtime.
We must be back **by** 12 o'clock.
Lunch will be served **from** 12 **to/until** 2. Can we meet **during** the lunch hour.

After, before, from ... to, by, until, during, since:

after ⎫	
before ⎪	may also be used as
since ⎬	conjunctions
until ⎭	

by (= no later than)

during (not to be confused grammatically with **while**, which is a conjunction, although both have the same meaning, e.g. during lunch = while we were having lunch)

NOTES
When we are measuring time, the adverb **ago** is also very important, e.g. I arrived here three days ago.
    Note that this emphasizes the arrival in the past, and is not quite the same as I have been here for three days, which emphasizes the length of a stay which is still continuing.

4.5.18.3 Other prepositions

What are you talking **about?**
Tell me **about** your holidays.
I couldn't do my homework **because of** the power cut.
Let's go **by** underground, **by** tram ...
(but: **on** foot)
They played **in spite of** the bad weather.
He looks **like** his father.
I'm talking to you **as** your friend.

about (a subject, topic of conversation, etc.)

because of (NB do not confuse this preposition grammatically with the conjunction **because**, e.g. because of the rain yesterday = because it was raining yesterday)

by (forms of transport; agents in the *passive*)

in spite of (also **despite**) This is a preposition with the same meaning as the conjunction **even though**, e.g. We played in spite of the rain. (= We played even though it rained.)

like (= similar to, in the same way as)

as (= because I am, etc.)

COMMUNICATIVE SITUATIONS

In the earlier part of the book we talked often about the way sentences and phrases were used in speech or writing. Our starting point was always the sentences and phrases themselves, beginning with a description of their form. Now we shall look at things from a different viewpoint, and in this final section present, under the headings of various common functions, a number of ways in which each them can be expressed. Note, however, that most of the important information in section 3.17, on the ways in which modal verbs serve various communicative purposes, will *not* be repeated here.

5.1 Greetings and leave taking

> 'Good morning
> 'Good afternoon, } Mr Smith.'
> 'Good evening,

When we meet people, we greet them according to the time of day. Three different times of day are recognized for this purpose: **morning** (until lunchtime); **afternoon** (from lunch until about 6 o'clock); **evening** (from about 6 o'clock until bedtime).

> 'Morning, Charles.'

In very casual situations, e.g. among workmates or friends, this shortened form of **Good morning** is sometimes heard.

> 'Hello, Bill.'
> 'Hi, Mary.'

These expressions may be used as greetings when we meet friends at any time of day. **Hello** is also the usual expression when we greet an (as yet unknown) caller on the telephone.

> A to B: 'Have you met Mr Smith?'
> B to Smith: 'No, not yet. **How do you do**? My name is Black.'
> Smith to B: '**How do you do**, Mr Black.'

How do you do? is the formal greeting used by *both* speakers when they are introduced to each other for the first time.

Although it looks and sounds like a question, it should never be answered, i.e. do not confuse it with **How are you**? which is a real question about health, etc.

129

Smith to Black:	'Oh, **how ARE you**, Mr Black?'
Black:	'Fine, thank you. **How are YOU**?'
Smith:	'I'm all right, thank you.

'Oh, I can't grumble.'

'Hello, I'm Sally.'
'Hi, Sally. **Nice to meet you**. I'm Jane.'

How are you? is usually said to people we already know quite well, i.e. we don't use it when we are first introduced. Usually it is simply a greeting, and is only repeated by the second speaker, not answered. But with high intonation it may function as a real enquiry about health, or a person's general situation, i.e. is he very busy, enjoying his work, has he been on holiday, is he making money, etc. Among close friends we also hear the form **How are things**? or even **How's things**? Typical answers are **Fine, thanks**./**All right**./**OK, thanks**. (With British speakers, allowance has to be made for their manner. They are brought up traditionally to be reserved, and also to understate. So a man who has just made a million pounds may answer How's things? with Oh, I can't grumble (in a tone of voice that suggests he is very pleased with life, and invites you to ask about his success): whilst someone who has just lost his house in a fire, may reply Oh, things could be worse, I suppose. in a voice which betrays how sorry he feels for himself!)

Especially when the young generation meet, introductions are less formal. **Nice to meet you**! replaces **How do you do**? Often even **Hi**! will do.

'I must leave now: **goodbye**, everybody.'
'**Goodnight**, Uncle Jim.'

Goodbye is an expression which anyone can use when taking their leave, at any time except late at night. Avoid **Good day**; this is almost never used in modern English. **Goodnight** is used late at night, most commonly among members of a family or household when they go to bed.

People who know each other well, and especially young people and children, use a number of other expressions when they are leaving; **Bye** (a shortened form of **Goodbye**); also **Bye**, **Bye** (though this sounds rather childish); **Cheerio**; **See you** (**soon**).

5.2 Greetings and other polite remarks on the phone

If a private call is made, the person answering the phone often does so by saying only his or her own number. The caller is then expected to say **Hello**?, give his (or her) name and say what he or she wants. (Each of the numbers in the phone number is said separately, and the figure **0** is pronounced **oh**, e.g. **477610 = four-double seven-six-one-oh**. When the same number occurs twice in succession, we say **double** (**seven**), etc.)

The operator at the switchboard of a company or organization usually answers by giving its name. Unless you actually want to talk to the switchboard operator, you will need to ask for a connection: **Could you (please) put me through to** (Mr Green)? or **May I/Could I speak to ...** or **I'd like to speak to ...**

'National Automobile Club, central office, good morning.'

'Good morning. **Could you put me through to** Mr Bill Cagey, please?'

'Yes, certainly. **Hold the line, please.**'

If we have to ask the caller to wait while a connection is made, or someone else is fetched to the phone, we say **Hold the line, please**, or **Would you mind holding on a moment**? (I'll fetch him/her.)

The examples show a common way of ending a private phone call.

'Thank you for calling.'

'Not at all. It was nice talking to you. Goodbye.'

5.3 Greetings and closing remarks in letters

Dear Jane,
 It was great listening to your records of

The usual form of greeting in personal letters is **Dear** + first name: **Dear Jane**, **Dear Uncle Peter**, **Dear Mum**, etc. In America, **Dear Friend** or **Dear Friends** is also not uncommon.

If we know the name of the person we are writing to, but cannot call him or her a friend, we use **Dear Mrs Salt**, **Dear Miss Hill**, etc.

Note that if you are in doubt whether a woman is married or not, or if you think she prefers no notice to be taken of her status, you may use the title **Ms** instead of **Mrs** or **Miss**.

Dear Mr Bane,
 We were pleased to receive your order of 13 May

Sometimes we do not even know the name of the person we are writing to, and perhaps not even the sex. For example, if we are writing to the editor of a newspaper. We

Dear Sir,
    It seems to me that the problem of unemployment is

Yours faithfully.

W.M. Blue
Sales Department

Yours sincerely,

C.P. Smith

Love,
Mary

should then greet them with **Dear Sir** (for a man), **Dear Madam** (for a woman), or **Dear Sir or Madam** (if we cannot guess whether the person addressed is a man or a woman). If we are writing to a company (= a group of people), we use the plural, i.e. **Dear Sirs**. (Americans often use **Gentlemen** as a greeting in this business situation.)

The usual closing greeting in a BrE letter, i.e. like **Goodbye** in a conversation, is **Yours sincerely** (for a letter which begins **Dear Jane**, **Dear Mr Hobson**, etc.) or **Yours faithfully** (for a letter which begins **Dear Sir**, etc.). The common equivalents in AmE letters are **Very sincerely yours** and **Very truly yours**. Letters to members of the family and close friends of any age often end with **Love**, **Love from**, or **Lots of love**, or **Yours ever**. Letters to a person we know well, though perhaps not a real friend, may end **With best wishes**, **Yours sincerely**.

Punctuation:
We usually write a comma after **Dear John**, etc. Nevertheless the first word of the text of the letter is written with a capital, as if it began a sentence, e.g. Dear John, Yesterday we went . . .

A British layout
Letter

19, Long Lane,
Hillsdon,
Surrey GF1 3BK

14ᵗʰ June 1985

Dear Mark,
    How are ...

            Yours sincerely,
                Algy

In both Britain and the USA there is more than one acceptable way of laying out a letter. The illustrations on the left show a typical layout from each country.

Envelope

Mr Mark Spicer,
Elm Cottage,
Minnows Green,
Nr. Oakshot,
Hants ST6 3VW

An American layout
Letter

4400 Ambler Boulevard
Smithville, ST 56789

January 12, 1985

Dear Amy,
Thank you...

        Very sincerely yours,
        Dwight

Envelope

Wilbur S. Grant
P.O. Box 414
424 Cuesta Real
La Honda
California 94020

                Mr & Mrs Darius Jones
                33A, 6 Ash St
                Cambridge
                Mass 02138

5.4 Attracting attention and addressing people

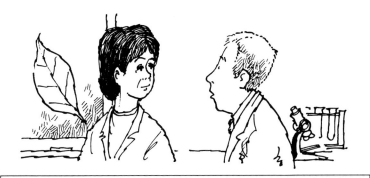

'**Excuse me**, could you explain the difference between a leaf and a bract?'

Saying **Excuse me** is a polite way of attracting someone's attention, and making sure they are listening to you, before you say what you really want to say. If you know the person's name, it is polite to add it, e.g. Excuse me, Mr Wells.

If you don't know the person's name, and you wish to be very formal, you may add **sir** (for a man), **madam** (for a woman), or **miss** (for a very young woman or girl, if you feel certain she isn't married). **Sir, madam** and **miss** are not used very much these days, except by sales assistants and waiters to customers, policemen to members of the public, airline hostesses to passengers, etc.

'**Excuse me, sir,** do you realize this is a no parking area?'
– 'Yes, **officer,** I'm not parking. I've run out of petrol.'

It is sometimes impolite and often incorrect to address people by the names of the jobs they do, e.g. **waiter, waitress, policeman, stewardess**. It is safest to use no title at all; but it is all right to address a policeman or policewoman as **officer;** and the attention of a waitress or stewardess might be attracted by saying **Excuse me, miss**.

'**Excuse me,** could I have the bill, please?'

'**Pardon me,** madam, I think you're standing on my foot!'

Pardon me is a rather more formal way of attracting attention.

5.5 Inviting people

'**Would you like** to come to my party?'
– 'I'd love to. Thank you very much.'
– 'I'd love to. But I'm afraid I can't.'

Modal auxiliary verbs play an important part in making offers or inviting people (see 3.17). Even routine invitations are phrased as questions, leaving the invited person free to answer **yes** or **no**.

Dentist: 'I shall need to see you once more to polish your teeth.
        Would you like to come back in a week's time?'

'**Perhaps you'd like** a drink with us?'
– 'Oh, thank you, that's very kind of you.'

If we use *adverbs* like **perhaps, maybe,** we can make the listener feel even more free to answer as he pleases.

'Take a seat, **please.**'
'You can sit here, **if you like.**'
'Have a look at this paper, **will you?**'

Imperatives are softened by the addition of **please** and sound like friendly invitations. We can also soften imperatives by adding **if you like, if you wish** or **will you?** (see 1.2.4).

5.6 Requesting and persuading

'Excuse me, **may** I interrupt you **just a second?**'
– 'Yes, of course.'
'**Could** you hold this for me?'
– 'Certainly, just a second.'

Modal auxiliary verbs are also used in most friendly or polite requests (see 3.17.3).

Just a second is used to make the interruption, or delay in answering a request, seem as short as possible.
  But don't think you will always have to wait only 'just a second' if someone asks you to. You may have to wait several minutes!

'*Can we have our ball back?*'

'I wonder if you would ⎫
'Could you   ⎬ do me a (small) favour?'
– 'Yes, what is it?' (The final answer will probably be yes.)
– 'Yes, I'll try.' (The final answer will probably be yes.)
– 'It depends what it is.' (The final answer may well be no.)

Sometimes we preface a specific request with a general request for help, by 'asking for a favour'.

'It's very hot in here. **Would you mind opening** a window?'
– 'No, not at all.'

More formal and more polite ways of making a request are **Would you mind** + *ing* form? and **Would you be so kind as to** + *base form* of a verb.

'**Would you be so kind as to** carry my bag for me?
– 'Yes, of course.'

'**Couldn't you** stay until tomorrow?'
'**Wouldn't you** like to meet Uncle Jim?'

Negative questions with *modal auxiliary verbs* (see 1.4.4) are the mark of a very strong attempt to persuade someone to do something, as they anticipate a positive answer.

'**Do take** another piece of cake! There is still plenty there. And you **must** try the shortbread, it's delicious.'

The *emphatic imperative*, i.e. **Do** + *base form* of a verb, and **must** + *base form* of a verb, also mark very strong attempts to persuade (see 1.3.1 and 3.13.1).

5.7 Apologizing

'Ouch! That's my foot you stepped on!'
– '**I'm very sorry**! I didn't notice that you were behind me.'

'You are sitting on my hat!'
– '**I beg your pardon**, Madam; I didn't see it in this dark corner.'

Complete sentences like **I'm very sorry** or **I beg your pardon** are only used when a very deep apology is needed. They sound quite formal, especially in the case of **I beg your pardon**. Alternatives include: **I'm really terribly sorry** and **Do please forgive me**.

'**Sorry** I'm late. I missed a train.'
– 'It's all right. We haven't started yet.'
'Is it the 9.20 that stops at Leeds, or is it the 10.15?'
– '**Pardon**?'
– 'I said, is it the 9.20 that . . .'

The shortened form **Sorry**! sounds less heavy. **Pardon**?, used on its own, is an apologetic request for someone to repeat something you have not heard properly. Intonation naturally plays an important part in showing how deep we intend an apology to be, and so do our gestures and the expressions on our faces.

Pardon me and **Excuse me** are used to attract attention (see 5.4). Don't use **Excuse me** as an apology; it isn't one.

Words like **apologize** and **regret** are sometimes used in writing, but are rarely heard in speech.

```
Dear Sir,
        We must apologize for the delay
in sending back your photographs. We regret
to say that the negatives were damaged during
processing.
```

5.8 Protesting and complaining

> **Must you** always play your radio when I'm working?
> **Do you have to** play it so loudly?
> Is it absolutely necessary to have it on now?
> Pop music can be very disturbing, you know.

Protests and complaints are usually made in an indirect or oblique way, using *modal auxiliaries*, and by asking questions rather than making statements.

5.9 Refusing, regretting and declining

We may refuse, rather than agree to do what someone requests. We may decline, with or without regrets, rather than accept an invitation. An excuse is often added.

Refusing

> Will you come back again tomorrow, please?
> – No, I'm sorry, I { won't. / can't. } I'm too busy.
> Dad, John would like to talk to you about our wedding plans.
> – Wedding plans? I'm not { going / ready / willing } to talk to him on that subject.
> It's no use asking me to change my mind. { I'm not going to. / I won't do it. }

Declining (with optional regrets and excuses)

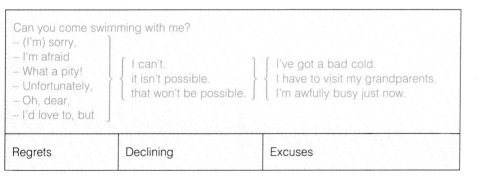

Regrets	Declining	Excuses
Can you come swimming with me? – (I'm) sorry, – I'm afraid – What a pity! – Unfortunately, – Oh, dear, – I'd love to, but	I can't. it isn't possible. that won't be possible.	I've got a bad cold. I have to visit my grandparents. I'm awfully busy just now.

5.10 Accusing and denying

Someone has been using my record player. It couldn't have been you, Charles, (by any chance), could it?

– No, sorry, { it wasn't me.
{ it must have been somebody else.

Charles, you used my record player, didn't you?

– I didn't, you know./Oh, no, I didn't.

It is usually uncomfortable and embarrassing to accuse someone of having done something, even when we are sure they have done it. A strong accusation may bring out an equally strong denial or an angry confession; a gentler accusation will bring out a gentler denial, or make confession easier. In the example, high falling intonation on the question tag, **didn't you?** would make the accusation stronger and more confident, while rising intonation would do the opposite.

Even when we are certain who the guilty person is, it may ease matters to pretend there is some doubt, as in the first example.

5.11 Warning

Look out! The wall's going to collapse!
Watch out – there's a rat under that pile of wood!
Be careful – you're going to drop that ice cream on your clothes!
Mind your head!
If you take your ring off, you'll probably forget to pick it up again.

When there is immediate danger, we need to use as few words as possible, and then *imperatives* are best.

When the danger is less immediate, *conditional sentences* are commonly used to give warnings (see also 3.17.5).

Appendix 1 Irregular verbs

(ed) means that the regular form in **ed** is an alternative to the irregular form.

Base	Past simple	Past perfect	Base	Past simple	Past perfect
arise	arose	have arisen	feel	felt	have felt
awake	awoke	have awoken	fight	fought	have fought
bear*	bore	have borne	find	found	have found
beat	beat	have beaten	flee	fled	have fled
become	became	have become	fly	flew	have flown
begin	began	have begun	forbid	forbade	have forbidden
bend	bent	have bent	forecast	forecast	have forecast
bet	bet	have bet	forget	forgot	have forgotten
bind	bound	have bound	forgive	forgave	have forgiven
bite	bit	have bitten	freeze	froze	have frozen
bleed	bled	have bled	get	got	have got
blow	blew	have blown	give	gave	have given
break	broke	have broken	go	went	have gone
breed	bred	have bred	grow	grew	have grown
bring	brought	have brought	hang	hung	have hung
broadcast	broadcast	have broadcast	hear	heard	have heard
build	built	have built	hide	hid	have hid/hidden
burn	burnt/burned	have burnt/burned	hit	hit	have hit
burst	burst	have burst	hold	held	have held
buy	bought	have bought	hurt	hurt	have hurt
cast	cast	have cast	keep	kept	have kept
catch	caught	have caught	kneel	knelt/kneeled	have knelt/kneeled
choose	chose	have chosen	knit	knit	have knit (ted)
cling	clung	have clung	know	knew	have known
come	came	have come	lay	laid	have laid
cost	cost	have cost	lead	led	have led
creep	crept	have crept	lean	leant/leaned	have leant/leaned
cut	cut	have cut	leap	leapt/leaped	have leapt/leaped
deal	dealt	have dealt	learn	learnt/learned	have learnt/learned
dig	dug	have dug	leave	left	have left
do	did	have done	lend	lent	have lent
draw	drew	have drawn	let	let	have let
dream	dreamt/dreamed	have dreamt/dreamed	lie	lay	have lain
			light	lit/lighted	have lit/lighted
drink	drank	have drunk	lose	lost	have lost
drive	drive	have driven	make	made	have made
eat	ate	have eaten	mean	meant	have meant
fall	fell	have fallen	meet	met	have met
feed	fed	have fed	pay	paid	have paid
			put	put	have put
			read	read	have read
			ride	rode	have ridden

bear is often used in the passive, with a different past participle, e.g. *I was born in 1980.*

Base	Past simple	Past perfect	Base	Past simple	Past perfect
ring	rang	have rung	spoil	spoilt/spoiled	have spoilt/spoiled
rise	rose	have risen	spread	spread	have spread
run	ran	have run	spring	sprang	have sprung
saw	sawed	have sawn (ed)	stand	stood	have stood
say	said	have said	steal	stole	have stolen
see	saw	have seen	stick	stuck	have stuck
seek	sought	have sought	sting	stung	have stung
sell	sold	have sold	stink	stank	have stunk
send	sent	have sent	strike	struck	have struck
set	set	have set	swear	swore	have sworn
sew	sewed	have sewn (ed)	sweep	swept	have swept
shake	shook	have shaken	swim	swam	have swum
shine	shone	have shone	swing	swung	have swung
shoot	shot	have shot	take	took	have taken
show	showed	have shown	teach	taught	have taught
shrink	shrank	have shrunk	tear	tore	have torn
shut	shut	have shut	tell	told	have told
sing	sang	have sung	think	thought	have thought
sink	sank	have sunk	throw	threw	have thrown
sit	sat	have sat	thrust	thrust	have thrust
sleep	slept	have slept	understand	understood	have understood
smell	smelt/smelled	have smelt/smelled	wake	woke	have woken
sow	sowed	have sown/sowed	wear	wore	have worn
speak	spoke	have spoken	weep	wept	have wept
speed	sped	have sped	win	won	have won
spend	spent	have spent	wind	wound	have wound
spin	spun	have spun	withdraw	withdrew	have withdrawn
spit	spat	have spat	write	wrote	have written
split	split	have split			

Appendix 2   Glossary of grammatical terms

This glossary concentrates mainly on terms which are not defined in the text itself, or terms which occur in many places but are defined in only one of them. Complete example sentences are printed in colour with the grammatical feature picked out in **bold type**. After the example(s), a short explanation draws attention to the featured part's relationship to the other parts of the sentence.

apposition	Sophia Loren, **the famous Italian filmstar**, will be on the show next week.
	The words in **bold type** are in *apposition* to 'Sophia Loren'. They are another way of describing her, or give us more information about her. The connection is made, in writing, simply by placing a comma on each side of the words in *apposition*. In speaking, we would pause slightly at each of these commas.
attributive	**Black** tulips are common, but I've never seen a **black** rose.
	An adjective is *attributive* when we put it in front of the noun which it describes.
base form of verb	The verb **go** is irregular.
	The *base form* of a verb is what you find it under in your dictionary.
base noun	Turn left at the first traffic **lights** after the bus **station**.
	We make some *compound nouns* by placing two nouns together. The second noun of the pair is the *base noun*; the first noun acts as a descriptive word, like an adjective or adjectival phrase, e.g. **traffic lights** are 'lights for the traffic (to obey)' and **a bus station** is 'a station for buses'.
clause	(1a) **Roses are red** and/but (1b) **violets are blue.** (1) **Read the words** (2) **which are written on the board.** (2) **When I see that book** (1) **I shall buy it.** (2) **Having no money on me** (1) **I couldn't buy anything to eat.**
	Part of a sentence which could stand as a sentence on its own, or which we can easily change into one because all the necessary parts of a sentence are represented in it.

143

Two *clauses* may be joined together by a *conjunction*, e.g. **and**, **but**, **when** in the examples. They may also be joined by changing the forms of words, e.g. **which** (= words), or by leaving words out as well, e.g. **Having** (= Because I had).

Two clauses in a sentence may be equal (e.g. 1a and 1b linked by **and/but**); or one of them (= 2, the dependent clause) may add to the meaning of the other (= 1, the main clause).

complement	We are **the champions**! She has become **my best friend** recently. The target of the verbs **be**, **become** (and some other verbs with similar meaning) is called a *complement*, not a *direct object* (see below).
compound noun	see: *base noun*
conjunction	I'm not going **because** I'm tired. A word which joins *clauses* to make a two-clause sentence.
dependent clause	see: *clause*
direct object	John hit **the ball** with his hand. I've broken **my watch**! Did you see **her** last night? The *direct object* is the target of the verb in a sentence. It may be a noun or a *pronoun*. Some verbs, e.g. **hit**, lack sufficient meaning if they are not given a *direct object*. These verbs are called 'transitive' and are marked v.t. in your dictionary. If we use an intransitive verb (marked v.i.), however, our sentence may not contain a *direct object*, e.g. The goldfish has died (no *direct object*).
direct speech	'**What's the matter with you**?' I asked. *Direct speech* means the words someone really said. They are written down between inverted commas.
exclamation	'We're going to the circus tonight.' 'Are we? **What fun**!' *Exclamations* are usually short and often not full sentences. They show surprise, pleasure, excitement or shock. In writing, we signal an *exclamation* by putting an exclamation mark (!) after it.

imperative	**Take** a taxi – it's quicker. **Don't spend** all your money! When we use the base form of a verb to give advice or instructions, we call it the *imperative*.
indirect objects	Shall I give **your mother** the key? I'm going to write a letter **to the newspaper** about this! Send **me** all your news, won't you? The *indirect object* is not the target of the verb alone, but of the verb and the *direct object* combined. It may be a noun or a *pronoun*. Its position may be between the verb and the *direct object*, or added to the *direct object* with a *preposition* (normally **to**).
indirect speech	I said **I am feeling ill**. I asked **what was the matter with him**. In *indirect speech* we report words that have been said previously. They may be the same as when they were first spoken (first example), or they may be changed (second example). In writing, no inverted commas are used.
infinitive	I want **to see** you very much. You'd better **come** at any time you like. **To dance** is fun, if you've got a good partner. In form, the *infinitive* is the same as the *base form of the verb* (see above), but in some circumstances the *preposition* **to** is added. We refer to the '*infinitive with to*' and the '*infinitive without to*'.
infinitive clause	'**To dance is fun**' (see next section above) is an *infinitive clause*.
main clause	see *clause*
negative	There's **not** much time now. Do**n't** touch that wire! These animals **never** eat meat. Sentences which contain **not** (short form **n't**) or **never** are *negative*.
object	see *direct object*, *indirect object*.
particle	When does school break **up**? It breaks **up** on December 19th.

A *particle* is a small word (normally a word you can also use as a *preposition*) which we add to a verb to give it a new meaning. It belongs to the verb, not to any noun which may follow it.

A verb with a *particle* added is called a *phrasal verb*.

phrasal verb   If you're not pleased with the goods, **bring** them **back**.
Please **take care of** this book.
Take it easy! We've got plenty of time.

A *phrasal verb* is a verb whose meaning depends on some words which follow it. The additional word or words may include *prepositions*, nouns, adjectives or *particles* (see next section above).

predicate   I **am David**.
None of these animals **has a tail**.
At this time of the year the trees **have lost all their leaves**.

The *predicate* is all the rest of a sentence after its *subject* has been taken away.

predicative   None of these tulips is **black**.

An adjective is *predicative* when the noun which it describes is the *subject* of a form of the verb **be**, and the adjective follows the verb.

(compare: *attributive*)

preposition   Look at the book **on** the table.
She ran **out of** the door.

One or more small words before a noun (or pronoun) which show the relationship between this noun and a preceding one (in this case the *preposition* begins an adjectival phrase); or between this noun and the preceding verb (in this case it begins an adverbial phrase).

pronoun   If **you** lend **me** your pen, I'll use **it** carefully.

A word used instead of repeating a noun, i.e. in the example **it** (= your pen). This *pronoun* is a direct object. In the example, the *pronoun* **you** is a subject, and the *pronoun* **me** an *indirect object*.

question	1 **What** are you doing? **Why** doesn't she like it? 2 **Will you** have tea or coffee? 3 **Are those** your gloves? **Did you** have a good holiday? 4 You're good at singing, **aren't you**?

Questions are indicated by the use of the question mark (?) at the end. They are of four main kinds: 1 **Wh**-questions, 2 alternative questions, 3 **Yes/No** questions, 4 tag questions.

sentence

Subject	(Aux)+Verb	(Object)	(Adverbial)
My sister	can sing sings	(pop songs)	(well). (at the weekends).

A *sentence* is made up of a *subject* and a *predicate*.

The minimum requirement for a *sentence* is normally a *subject* and, as *predicate*, a verb which agrees with it in person and number (singular or plural).

There are a few exceptions, e.g. What about you? has no verb, and *imperatives* usually do not have *subjects*, e.g. Have a good time!

statement

Some boys were climbing a mountain. (+)
They weren't wearing climbing boots. (−)

A *statement* is a *sentence* which gives a fact, i.e. which is not a *question* or an *imperative* or an *exclamation*. It may be positive (+) or negative (−).

subject

I am David.
None of these animals has a tail.
At this time of the year **the trees** have lost all their leaves.
That lamp-post was knocked over by a car.

In the active, the *subject* is the person or thing responsible for the action which a verb describes. In the passive, it is the person or thing which has that action done to it.

INDEX

This index includes grammatical terms (in *italic type*), English words and phrases (in **bold type**), and communicative situations and purposes (normal type). The numbers refer to the sections (not the page numbers) in which the items occur.